Home Run Kings

Other Books in the History Makers Series:

America's Founders

Artists of the Renaissance

Cartoonists

Civil War Generals of the Confederacy

Civil War Generals of the Union

Cult Leaders

Dictators

Fighters Against American Slavery

Gangsters

Great Authors of Children's Literature

Great Composers

Great Conquerors

Gunfighters

Leaders of Ancient Greece

Leaders of Black Civil Rights

Magicians and Illusionists

Male Olympic Champions

Native American Chiefs and Warriors

Presidential Assassins

Rulers of Ancient Egypt

Rulers of Ancient Rome

Scientists of Ancient Greece

Serial Killers

Twentieth-Century American Writers

Women Leaders of Nations

Women of the American Revolution

*History*MAKERS

Home Run Kings

By Michael V. Uschan

Lucent Books
P.O. Box 289011, San Diego, CA 92198-9011

For my grandmother Helen "Lena" Uschan, an immigrant from Austria who came to love her adopted country's national pastime and became a rabid fan of the Milwaukee Braves and Brewers.

On Cover: *Sammy Sosa and Mark McGwire (background), Roger Maris (bottom right), George Herman "Babe" Ruth Jr. (bottom left).*

Library of Congress Cataloging-in-Publication Data

Uschan, Michael V., 1948–
    Home run kings / by Michael V. Uschan.
        p.   cm. — (History makers)
    Includes bibliographical references (p.) and index.
    Summary: Discusses the careers of several baseball stars known for their home run hitting, including Babe Ruth, Roger Maris, Hank Aaron, Mark McGwire, and Sammy Sosa.
    ISBN 1-56006-636-9 (lib. bdg. : alk. paper)
    1. Baseball players—United States—Biography—Juvenile literature. 2. Home runs (Baseball)—Juvenile literature. [1. Baseball players. 2. Home runs (Baseball)] I. Title. II. Series.
    GV865.A1 U83   2000
    796.357'092'2—dc21
    [B]
                                                                99-053008
                                                                CIP

Copyright 2000 by Lucent Books, Inc.
P.O. Box 289011, San Diego, California 92198-9011

Printed in the U.S.A.

CONTENTS

FOREWORD   6

INTRODUCTION
From the "Babe" to "Big Mac"   8

CHAPTER 1
Baseball: The National Pastime   12

CHAPTER 2
Babe Ruth: The Greatest Player Ever   23

CHAPTER 3
Roger Maris: Battling the Legend of the Babe   36

CHAPTER 4
Hank Aaron: Breaking a Record and Defeating Bigotry   48

CHAPTER 5
Mark McGwire: Chasing Roger and the Babe   60

CHAPTER 6
Sammy Sosa: Happy with 66!   73

EPILOGUE
Home Run "Déjà Vu"   85

Notes   91
Chronology   98
For Further Reading   101
Works Consulted   102
Index   106
Picture Credits   112
About the Author   112

FOREWORD

The literary form most often referred to as "multiple biography" was perfected in the first century A.D. by Plutarch, a perceptive and talented moralist and historian who hailed from the small town of Chaeronea in central Greece. His most famous work, *Parallel Lives*, consists of a long series of biographies of noteworthy ancient Greek and Roman statesmen and military leaders. Frequently, Plutarch compares a famous Greek to a famous Roman, pointing out similarities in personality and achievements. These expertly constructed and very readable tracts provided later historians and others, including playwrights like Shakespeare, with priceless information about prominent ancient personages and also inspired new generations of writers to tackle the multiple biography genre.

The Lucent History Makers series proudly carries on the venerable tradition handed down from Plutarch. Each volume in the series consists of a set of five to eight biographies of important and influential historical figures who were linked together by a common factor. In *Rulers of Ancient Rome*, for example, all the figures were generals, consuls, or emperors of either the Roman Republic or Empire; while the subjects of *Fighters Against American Slavery*, though they lived in different places and times, all shared the same goal, namely the eradication of human servitude. Mindful that politicians and military leaders are not (and never have been) the only people who shape the course of history, the editors of the series have also included representatives from a wide range of endeavors, including scientists, artists, writers, philosophers, religious leaders, and sports figures.

Each book is intended to give a range of figures—some well known, others less known; some who made a great impact on history, others who made only a small impact. For instance, by making Columbus's initial voyage possible, Spain's Queen Isabella I, featured in *Women Leaders of Nations*, helped to open up the New World to exploration and exploitation by the European powers. Unarguably, therefore, she made a major contribution to a series of events that had momentous consequences for the entire world. By contrast, Catherine II, the eighteenth-century Russian queen, and Golda Meir, the modern Israeli prime minister, did not play roles of global impact; however, their policies and actions significantly influenced the historical development of both their own countries and their regional neighbors. Regardless of their relative importance in the greater historical scheme, all of the figures chronicled in the History Makers series made contributions to posterity; and their public achievements, as well as what is known about their private lives, are presented and evaluated in light of the most recent scholarship.

In addition, each volume in the series is documented and substantiated by a wide array of primary and secondary source quotations. The primary source quotes enliven the text by presenting eyewitness views of the times and culture in which each history maker lived; while the secondary source quotes, taken from the works of respected modern scholars, offer expert elaboration and/or critical commentary. Each quote is footnoted, demonstrating to the reader exactly where biographers find their information. The footnotes also provide the reader with the means of conducting additional research. Finally, to further guide and illuminate readers, each volume in the series features photographs, two bibliographies, and a comprehensive index.

The History Makers series provides both students engaged in research and more casual readers with informative, enlightening, and entertaining overviews of individuals from a variety of circumstances, professions, and backgrounds. No doubt all of them, whether loved or hated, benevolent or cruel, constructive or destructive, will remain endlessly fascinating to each new generation seeking to identify the forces that shaped their world.

From the "Babe" to "Big Mac"

In 1918 Boston Red Sox manager Ed Barrow made a decision that changed baseball forever. Barrow's Red Sox were so weak offensively that Harry Hooper, one of his coaches, suggested he use a hard-hitting young pitcher as an everyday player. In the club's first spring training game, the pitcher played first base and slugged two home runs. In the regular season opener at the Polo Grounds in New York City, he was the winning pitcher and launched a tremendous homer that sailed out of the cavernous ballpark. That's when Hooper recommended Barrow insert him in the daily lineup. Barrow, an old-fashioned person who wore a suit and a soft straw hat instead of a uniform while managing, reacted in shock: "I'd be the laughingstock of baseball if I changed the best left-hander in the game into an outfielder."[1] But Barrow had invested $50,000 in the Red Sox; he not only wanted the team to win but to draw big crowds so it would make money. And fans were turning out in huge numbers just to see his pitcher hit.

So on May 6, 1918, three years to the day after the player hit his first major league home run, Barrow started him at first base against the New York Yankees. He hit his second home run in two games and smashed his third the next day, a remarkable feat in an era of few home runs.

The pitcher's name was George Herman "Babe" Ruth Jr.

The Home Run as Theater

Baseball historian Donald Honig claims that Ruth "virtually in-

Power hitter Babe Ruth was converted from a pitcher into an everyday player.

vented the home run, or at least the home run as a piece of theater."[2] Ruth's monstrous drives had sportswriters thumbing through their thesauruses for dramatic verbs to describe the act: *blasted, clouted, crushed, slammed, muscled, poked, propelled, walloped.*

Before Ruth started smashing record numbers of home runs, the long ball king had been Frank "Home Run" Baker of the Philadelphia Athletics, who for four seasons starting in 1911 either tied or finished first in the American League (AL) home run race. But Baker never hit more than a dozen in one season, and in 1917 the Yankees' Wally Pipp captured the AL crown with just nine.

When Ruth began playing regularly in 1918, he hit 11 to tie with Philadelphia's Tilly Walker. In 1919 Ruth exploded for a major league record of 29 homers and the next year nearly doubled that to 54—more home runs than all but one of the fifteen other major league *teams* hit that season!

Thus was born the Home Run King, the most idolized player in a game that had previously relied on bunts, stolen bases, and clusters of singles and doubles to score runs. In making the home run fashionable, Ruth made the game more exciting, creating hundreds of thousands of new fans and ushering in a dramatic new era. In *The King of Swat*, William F. McNeil explains why home run hitters became baseball's biggest stars:

> He towers over his compatriots like the Colossus of Rhodes. The clear, sharp impact as hardwood meets cowhide—the small, white pellet whistling skyward into the night— 50,000 fans leaving their seats in unison as the baseball settles into the far distant grandstand for a game-winning home run. This is the single most exciting and dramatic act in baseball. Hitters who could propel baseballs long distances have been idolized by men and women everywhere.[3]

Breaking Ruth's Records

When Ruth retired in 1935, his 60 home runs in 1927 and 714 career long balls became the most sacred records in baseball. But when players neared Ruth's records they discovered something odd: even though he had died in 1948, Ruth was still as revered as when he was hitting balls out of Yankee Stadium.

While Yankee slugger Roger Maris hit 61 home runs in 1961 to better the Babe by one, he received hate mail saying he was not good enough to take Ruth's place in the record books. His season of glory became a torturous struggle that created controversy and made

Maris so nervous patches of his hair fell out. When Maris hit number 61, Baseball Commissioner Ford Frick cheapened the feat by claiming Maris had not broken Ruth's record, set in 154 games, because the 1961 season had been lengthened to 162 games. Biased because he had been a friend of Ruth's, Frick ordered record books to include that unholy distinction.

In 1974 when Henry Aaron of the Atlanta Braves smashed his record 715th home run, he felt more relief than pure elation. Like Maris, Aaron received hate mail saying he was unworthy to surpass Ruth. This time letter writers were upset about the color of this African American's skin, not his undisputed credentials as a great player.

Although Maris and Aaron both broke Ruth's records, the controversy and bitter feelings that swirled around them squeezed the joy from their accomplishments.

The Greatest Home Run Year Ever

But in 1998 Mark McGwire of the St. Louis Cardinals and Sammy Sosa of the Chicago Cubs brought joy, drama, and one of

The exemplary sportsmanship exhibited by Sammy Sosa (left) and Mark McGwire (right) ensured that their competition for the single-season home run record would not be marred by issues like racism.

the rarest of all commodities in sports—genuine respect and sportsmanship between two fierce competitors—to baseball's most exciting home run chase ever. McGwire did not just break Maris's record; he obliterated it with 70 home runs while Sosa tallied 66.

Former catcher Tim McCarver, now one of baseball's finest broadcast analysts, writes that the way these baseball gladiators conducted themselves ennobled their season-long quest:

> They wouldn't dignify questions about their homer race having racial overtones and the notion that some fans were favoring one over the other based solely on skin color or heritage [McGwire is white, Sosa a black from the Dominican Republic]. They became each other's greatest champions. Sosa would tell reporters that McGwire would be the home-run king because: "He's the man." McGwire [talked] about Sosa's "unbelievable class" and remarked how he hoped they both passed Maris and shared the new record when the season ended. America had rarely seen such sportsmanship, brotherhood, humility, and class wrapped in a competitive cocoon.[4]

More importantly than breaking the record, their glorious season dispelled the ill will that for years had clouded the achievements of Maris and Aaron. And once and for all, McGwire and Sosa put to rest the lingering, ghostlike presence of the Babe, who had haunted pursuers of his records for more than a half century.

CHAPTER 1

Baseball: The National Pastime

Baseball is considered America's great national pastime, the one game everyone can play and enjoy from major leaguers making millions of dollars to small children in T-ball who try to emulate the sport's greatest stars. In *Baseball America*, Donald Honig claims the game is universally loved because of its simple, primitive appeal:

> The lure of baseball? The charm? The magic? Hold a ball in your hand and your instinct is to throw it; grip a stick in your hand and your desire is to hit that ball; be some distance away and your need is to catch that ball; and if you are a spectator, then you won't move a muscle or blink an eye until you have seen who wins the race—the ball plunging toward earth or the man who is trying to prevent that from happening. With unending renewal the ritual goes on and on, for there will be, in Carl Sandburg's phrase, "Always the young strangers who will come to try it anew."[5]

Baseball's Humble Beginnings

After gaining independence from Great Britain in the Revolutionary War, Americans forged new traditions in almost every area of their lives, including the games they played. Baseball is descended from cricket and rounders, British games that involved a ball, a bat, a level playing field, and stations that players advanced to in order to score.

By the end of the eighteenth century, Americans were playing several primitive forms of baseball; one called "one old cat" or "one o'cat" was popular in New York City, a key breeding ground for the sport. Most variations involved a square field with stakes at the corners serving as stations and a hitter's box midway between the first and fourth stations. By 1835 other games known as "town ball" and "New York ball" were played in larger eastern cities. In those early years the pitcher was called a "bowler" and the hitter the "sticker," terms borrowed from British games.

Around 1840 sand-filled sacks were substituted for stakes and became known as bases, giving birth to a new name for the game—baseball. Although the term was first used in England for a children's game, historians claim that the first game of the sport known today as baseball was played on June 19, 1846, in Hoboken, New Jersey, when the Knickerbocker Baseball Club lost to the New York Nine, with the losers buying dinner for the winners.

The founder of the Knickerbockers and of the game itself was Alexander Joy Cartwright, who was born April 17, 1820, in New York, and died July 12, 1892, in Honolulu, Hawaii, after carrying baseball to the islands that in 1959 would become the fiftieth state. Elected in 1938 to the Baseball Hall of Fame, his plaque in Cooperstown, New York, reads:

> Alexander Cartwright is called "The Father of Modern Baseball." Using his ability as an engineer and draftsman, he ingeniously located the bases 90 feet apart. His rules

The game of baseball evolved from British games such as rounders and cricket (pictured).

also established 9 innings as a game and 9 players as a team. He provided for three outs per side, set an unalterable batting order, and eliminated throwing the ball at a runner to retire him. Cartwright organized the first team—the New York Knickerbockers in 1845.[6]

A controversy developed in the early years of the twentieth century over whether Cartwright or Abner Doubleday originated baseball. In 1907 the Mills Commission credited Doubleday with establishing the game's basic rules, mainly because it wanted baseball associated with a war hero. A graduate of the U.S. Military Academy, Doubleday helped defend Fort Sumter in the first battle of the Civil War.

Although later research proved Cartwright invented the game, the Hall of Fame was located in Doubleday's hometown as a tribute to his contributions to baseball.

Baseball Becomes Popular

A story associated with Abraham Lincoln shows how much the game's popularity had grown in the years leading up to the Civil War, which began in 1861. When Republicans arrived in Springfield, Illinois, on May 18, 1860, to notify Lincoln he had been nominated for president, he was not home; a messenger found him playing baseball in the town commons. "Tell the gentlemen," Lincoln said, "that I am glad to know of their coming; but they'll have to wait a few minutes 'till I make another base hit."[7]

The anecdote may be no truer than claims that young George Washington could not lie to his father after chopping down a cherry tree. However, the fact that Lincoln was linked with baseball at this early stage of its evolution, even in myth, shows how quickly the game was becoming part of popular culture.

The Civil War introduced baseball to tens of thousands of soldiers, who played it in the long, dull periods between battles. On Christmas Day 1862, two squads made of star players from various Union army teams competed before an estimated 40,000 soldiers—a crowd that may have been the largest to see an athletic event in the nineteenth century.

Another Union game turned tragic when interrupted by an enemy attack. "Suddenly there came a scattering fire of which the three fielders caught the brunt," wrote soldier George H. Putnam. "The center field[er] was hit and was captured, the left and right field[ers] managed to get into our lines." The Northern soldiers drove back the Confederates but Putnam lamented, "We had lost not only our center field[er] but the only baseball in [Texas]."[8]

When the war ended, soldiers spread the game throughout the nation. In 1865 the *New York Clipper* reported that even defeated Southerners were embracing the sport: "Base ball fever is rapidly assuming the form of an epidemic among the constructed and unreconstructed denizens of [the Confederacy]."[9]

Professional Baseball

Baseball was strictly an amateur pursuit until after the Civil War. Athletes competed for the sheer pleasure they derived from the new game, which arrived at the collegiate level in July 1859 when Amherst College beat Williams College by the improbable score of 73–32. But as baseball continued to grow in popularity, it took on a new importance to its fans, who were no longer content with watching amateurs. Their desire to see great athletes engage in exciting, well-played games led to the rise of professional baseball.

The first professional team was the Cincinnati Red Stockings, a squad of athletic mercenaries formed by Harry Wright, a professional cricket player from England. In 1869 the team won seventy-nine of eighty games and tied another in a schedule of contests

The Cincinnati Red Stockings, the first professional baseball team, lost only one game in their first season.

that carried it from Long Island, New York, to San Francisco, California. The team's only loss came in their final game, 8–7 in eleven innings to the Brooklyn Atlantics.

Two years later the National Association of Professional Baseball Players was formed. But on February 2, 1876, a group of influential owners headed by William A. Hulbert of Chicago, unhappy with the way the Association was governed, founded the National League of Professional Baseball Clubs known today as the National League (NL). Boston beat Philadelphia 6–5 on April 22, 1876, in the first NL game played and the new circuit quickly put the National Association out of business.

Several rival leagues challenged the NL but none successfully until 1901 when former sportswriter Byron Banford Johnson and former player Charles Comiskey founded the American League (AL). Johnson and Comiskey were partly motivated by a desire to clean up baseball, which at the turn of the century had a reputation as unsavory as that of many of its players, who drank, gambled on games, and were viewed by polite society as roughnecks employed in a socially unacceptable profession. Baseball fans were not much better; rowdy behavior was common and spectators treated umpires brutally, taunting them over calls and sometimes threatening them by swinging a hangman's noose.

In *The American League,* authors John Stewart Bowman and Joel Zoss write:

> In those days, baseball had a reputation as a rough-and-ready sport. Players baited umpires as well as opposing players, and foul language was commonplace. Fistfights often broke out and intentional spiking [injuring opposing players with the spikes on their playing shoes] was not unheard of. It was not the environment thought to be fit for ladies of the Victorian era. Johnson and Comiskey agreed on the need to end the rowdiness, to discourage the sale of liquor in all parks, to stop the use of profanity, to instill respect for umpires and to encourage women's attendance. Part of their dream was a new image for the game.[10]

In the first AL game on April 24, 1901, the Chicago White Sox beat the Cleveland Bronchos (a team known today as the Indians) 8–2. In its inaugural season, the AL raided 111 players from the NL and in 1902 outdrew the senior league 2.2 million fans to 1.7 million.

Faced with such a powerful rival, the NL in 1903 accepted the upstart AL as an equal. The leagues signed an agreement in January 1903 that allocated territorial rights for sixteen franchises, set up a system of common schedules and rules, and created a World Series matching each league's champions. That fall in the first World Series, the AL Boston Pilgrims defeated the Pittsburgh Pirates by winning five of eight games.

Baseball's Color Line

Adrian "Cap" Anson was one of the great pioneers of baseball's early years, first as a player and starting in 1879 as manager of the NL Chicago White Stockings, a team known today as the Cubs. Anson won five league championships in his first seven years as manager and was one of the game's great innovators, originating the use of offensive and defensive signals to communicate with players and tactics such as the hit-and-run, in which a player on base runs as soon as a ball is pitched to a batter, who has been ordered to swing away.

But Anson, the first player with 3,000 career hits and a member of the Hall of Fame, was also a racist. In *A Complete History of the Negro Leagues,* Mark Ribowsky writes that "Anson became the point man in the drive to hound blacks out of the game."[11]

In the 1880s at least twenty African Americans played for white clubs, including George Stovey and brothers Moses Fleetwood Walker and William Welday Walker. In 1884 when Fleetwood pitched for a Toledo minor league team in an exhibition game against Chicago, Anson shouted "get that nigger off the field."[12] Three years later when the New York Giants decided to promote Stovey to the major leagues, Anson fought to bar African Americans, claiming the move was illegal. He mustered support and on July 14, 1887, members of the International League, composed of minor league teams, met in Buffalo, New York, and voted 6–4 to bar African Americans—the four "no" votes were from teams that had African American players. The headline the next day in the *Newark Daily Journal* read: "Color Line Drawn in Baseball."[13] The racial barrier remained in effect until April 15, 1947, when Jackie Robinson took the field for the Brooklyn Dodgers to become the first African American major league player since the color line had been drawn.

In response to the racial ban, African Americans organized their own teams, and in 1920 eight clubs formed the first of the Negro Leagues, which continued play through 1960 and produced many great stars like Josh Gibson, the "black Babe Ruth." Some accounts claim Gibson hit 75 home runs in one season and more

Jackie Robinson (far left) was the first African American to play in the major leagues since 1887, when baseball barred African Anericans.

than 800 for his career, but baseball historian William F. McNeil notes that because of poor record keeping, "it is often impossible to separate fact from fiction when discussing the fabled sluggers of the Negro Leagues."[14]

African American stars often fared well in exhibition games against white major leaguers. "We saw that our best was as good as their best. Then when the game was over, we'd go our way and they'd go theirs," said catcher Buck Leonard, one of the Negro League stars voted into the Hall of Fame after it began honoring them in 1971. "It was frustrating."[15]

The racist decision deprived African Americans of an opportunity to play major league baseball, diluted the game's talent pool for sixty years, and denied white fans the chance to see some of the greatest athletes who ever played the game.

The Game Evolves

Baseball today is far different from its early years because of changes in rules dating back to the end of the nineteenth century. It was not until 1884 that pitchers were allowed to throw overhand—some purists claim the sport did not really become *baseball* until then—and up until 1887 batters could request a high or low pitch, with the hurler only allowed to vary speed to fool the hitter. In 1887 the number of balls to walk a batter was reduced from nine to five and two years later dropped to four, today's standard. In 1888 the number of strikes to make the batter out fell from five to today's three.

One of the most revolutionary changes was to lengthen the distance between the pitching mound and home plate. In 1881 the mound was moved back five feet, putting it fifty feet away from home plate, and in 1893 the distance was increased to today's sixty feet, six inches. In 1893 the flat bat was also banned, requiring players to use rounded bats.

Most rule changes were designed to increase the pace of play and boost offense in a game that was low-scoring and often boring. But in *The King of Swat,* William F. McNeil claims the most significant factor in changing the game's essential nature was to introduce a ball that went farther when hit:

> Home runs were a rare commodity in the early days of baseball, primarily because of the poor quality of the balls and the outlandish dimensions of the ballparks. The balls were soft and poorly constructed compared to today's balls, and they did not travel nearly as far when hit. Additionally, only one ball was used in a game, and it became badly misshapen as the game progressed. The baseball fields themselves were often not enclosed, so long hits were always in play. It was a game of speed, with doubles and triples the fashion of the day.[16]

The first balls were soft, made of wound yarn with a leather cover. But in 1910 a ball with a cork center was introduced, and NL and AL hitting averages escalated a dozen points. The number of .300 hitters in both leagues increased from 16 to 43 and the average number of home runs for each team jumped from 19 to 31.

A player's average is based on the number of hits in all at bats; a .300 hitter, for example, gets three hits for every ten at bats. A .300 average is considered a mark of excellence, and in 1924 Rogers Hornsby of the St. Louis Cardinals hit .424, the highest season average in history.

But even with a charged-up ball, baseball was still a slow-paced, low-scoring game based on pitching, defense, and offense that relied on singles, doubles, walks, and stolen bases to score runs. Although home runs created runs quickly, managers favored the old-fashioned offensive strategy that shunned a reliance on raw power.

Ironically, it took a pitcher to make the home run popular and alter the game for all time. His name was George Herman "Babe" Ruth Jr.

The Original Home Run King

Ruth quickly became the game's best left-hander with the Boston Red Sox, but from his first minor league practice in 1914, it was Ruth's unbelievably long home runs that intrigued fans. *Baltimore American* writer Rodger Pippen, who roomed with Ruth during spring training, glorified the homer Ruth hit on March 7, 1914, in his first game as a professional:

> The next batter made a hit that will live in the memory of all who saw it. That clouter was George Ruth, the southpaw from St. Mary's school. The ball carried so far to right field that he walked around the bases. He crossed home plate before [the outfielder] picked up the ball in the cornfield that grew beyond the ballfield in deepest right.[17]

Ruth's homer was the longest ever struck in Fayetteville, North Carolina, where fans had bragged for several years about the long balls Jim Thorpe hit there. Ruth in his first game had outdone the great Olympic champion, who was now in the major leagues. Ruth only hit nine home runs in his first four seasons as a pitcher; but when he did connect, his high, incredibly long drives delighted fans who came to watch him.

The interest in Ruth and home runs in general did not escape the notice of baseball owners. After the "Black Sox" scandal involving Chicago White Sox players who accepted money to lose games in the 1919 World Series, owners tried to rejuvenate interest in baseball by changing rules for 1920 to promote home runs and offense. New rules prohibited pitchers from doctoring the ball (scraping, spitting on, or applying grease or tobacco juice to it) to make their pitches harder to hit and instructed umpires to remove scuffed balls from the game. In the past when one ball was used for an entire contest, it became soft or out of shape, making it difficult for players to hit it very far.

The effect of the new rules was compounded by what became known as the "lively ball." The A. J. Reach Company began using a new machine that wound yarn more tightly around its cork center, making balls travel farther and helping ignite another hitting boom. Commenting comically on the new lively ball, famed humorist Ring Lardner wrote:

> The master minds that controls baseball says to themselfs that if it is home runs that the public wants to see, why leave us give them home runs. So they fixed up a ball that if you don't miss it entirely it will clear the fence, and the result is that players which used to specialize in hump back liners to the pitcher is now amongst our leading sluggers.[18]

When he became a full-time player in 1919, Ruth hit a record 29 home runs and the next year nearly doubled that mark to 54.

The enthusiasm generated among fans by Ruth's long blasts led team owners to make rule changes that promoted more home runs.

The feat excited even the *Literary Digest*, which noted how Ruth had changed the game: "Babe Ruth not only has smashed all records, but he has smashed the long accepted system of things in the batting world, and on the ruins of that system has erected another system whose dominant quality is brute force."[19]

Thus was born the Home Run King.

CHAPTER 2

Babe Ruth: The Greatest Player Ever

It was a question Babe Ruth must have heard ten thousand times: How do you hit so many home runs? One of his answers not only explained his awesome power, it provided a valuable insight into his flamboyant personality:

> I swing as hard as I can, and I try to swing right through the ball. In boxing, your fist usually stops when you hit a man, but it's possible to hit so hard that your fist doesn't stop. I try to follow through in the same way. I swing big, with everything I've got. I hit big or I miss big. I like to live as big as I can.[20]

George Herman "Babe" Ruth Jr. did live "as big" as he could. Born February 6, 1895, to working-class parents in Baltimore, Maryland, Ruth became the biggest star baseball would ever know. His larger-than-life personality—from unbelievably long home runs to his equally legendary appetites for food, alcohol, and women—made him as famous in the 1920s and 1930s as basketball player Michael Jordan would be over a half century later.

Ruth was the heroic, mythical figure who in the 1932 World Series predicted he would hit a home run, and then had the power to fulfill his audacious boast. When queried in 1930 about making more money ($80,000 per year) than President Herbert Hoover, he blithely replied, "I had a better year than he did."[21] And when

Babe Ruth (pictured signing a figurine of himself) and his powerful swing soon became legendary.

Ruth was old and overweight in 1935, he hit three home runs in one game to give fans one final, golden memory of the first great home run hitter.

Baseball historian Donald Honig explains Ruth's mystique:

> If Babe Ruth had not been born, it would have been impossible to invent him. He was not just the premier left-handed pitcher of his time and the greatest home run hitter ever, but it was all packed into a booming, fun loving, perennially adolescent personality that would have brought tears to the eyes of [promoter] P. T. Barnum. He was a one man circus, born and molded to entertain, dominate, captivate, and altogether flourish in the imagination. Everything about Ruth was big, big, big, from the statistics to the personality to the impact. He was Moby Dick in a goldfish bowl.[22]

A Tough Little Kid

George Herman Ruth Sr. and Katherine Schamberger had eight children but only one other child survived infancy, Margaret, born in 1900 and nicknamed "Mamie." "Big George," as his father was known, ran a saloon in a rough area near Baltimore's waterfront while "Little George" grew up roaming those tough streets, getting into trouble and becoming impossible to control. "I was a bum as a kid,"[23] Ruth admitted. He once described his childhood:

> We lived in back of a saloon and my mother often tended bar when my father was away. I learned early to drink beer, wine, and whiskey, and I think I was about five when I first chewed tobacco. I didn't particularly like the taste, but I knew it was supposed to be bad. There was a lot of cussing in pop's saloon, so I learned a lot of swear words, some really bad ones. I think that's why they kept sticking me at St. Mary's.[24]

On June 13, 1902, his parents sent Ruth to St. Mary's Industrial School for Boys, a facility near Baltimore for orphans, children from broken homes, and juvenile delinquents run by the Roman Catholic Xaverian Brothers. Ruth was at St. Mary's for only a month and then another month the following November, but when sent back again in 1904, he lived there most of the next decade. His sister and mother visited every month, bringing baskets of fruit, candy, and cookies that Ruth shared with other boys.

It was at St. Mary's that Brother Matthias, whom Ruth called "the greatest man I ever knew,"[25] introduced him to the salvation of his life—baseball.

Ruth Learns Baseball

At St. Mary's, about eight hundred boys studied school subjects and industrial arts. Ruth learned carpentry, cigar making, and tailoring; even when rich and famous, he sewed new collars on his silk shirts. Brother Matthias, a huge man at six feet six inches and more than 250 pounds, taught him how to play baseball, but Ruth bragged, "I could hit the first time I picked up a bat."[26]

The left-handed Ruth first played catcher even though he had to use a right-handed glove, which he had to drop so he could throw after catching the ball. When Ruth criticized a pitcher, a Xaverian brother dared him to pitch and Ruth discovered it was "easy to strike out batters."[27] But it was always hitting that Ruth excelled at. His average was usually around .500 at St. Mary's, and Ruth was so good that in 1913 he began playing on weekends with local adult teams.

Newspaper stories brought Ruth to the attention of Jack Dunn, owner and manager of the minor league Baltimore Orioles. After watching Ruth strike out twenty-two batters in a 6–0 St. Mary's victory, in February 1914 Dunn signed the twenty-year-old to a contract for $100 a month for six months.

Ruth Gets His Nickname

When Ruth went to spring training, he was six feet two inches tall and a lean 180 pounds. Older players called him Dunn's "Babe," and when Baltimore sportswriter Rodger Pippen used it in his stories, one of sports' most cherished nicknames was born.

Every day seemed like Christmas morning to Ruth, who found new wonders everywhere and spent money lavishly. During the first few days of spring training, Ruth paid the elevator operator at the team's hotel so he could ride the elevator for hours and also bought his first bicycle, which he rode to practice. He amazed his teammates with how much he could eat, but his legendary appetite would later cause weight problems.

On April 22 when Ruth gave up only six hits and no runs to win his first regular season game, fewer than two hundred fans witnessed his debut. The Orioles were having trouble competing for fans with the Baltimore Terrapins of the new Federal League, which challenged the two other major leagues before folding in 1915 after two seasons.

Although Ruth won fourteen games, the Orioles were struggling financially and Dunn needed money. On July 10 he sold Ruth and two other players to the Boston Red Sox for $25,000. Ruth was in the major leagues four months after turning professional.

Pitching in Boston

The trio arrived in Boston on July 11, and Ruth pitched that day against Cleveland, leaving the game in the seventh inning after allowing two runs to tie the score 3–3. Boston won 4–3, but within a few weeks Ruth began to struggle and was demoted to minor league Providence (Rhode Island), where he won nine games. Recalled by Boston in September, Ruth beat the New York Yankees 11–5 and cracked his first major league hit, a double. Ruth's first season was promising as he compiled a 23–8 International League record for Baltimore and Providence and a 2–1 record with Boston.

The day Ruth reported to Boston, he ate breakfast at Lander's Coffee Shop and became enraptured by a pretty young waitress named Helen Woodford. Ruth kept eating there to romance

As a pitcher, Ruth (second from right) compiled a 2–1 record in his first year with Boston.

Woodford, and they were married on October 17. Even though he was not yet twenty-one and she was only seventeen, Ruth could afford to marry because he was making $3,500 a year, a great deal of money then.

Ruth won eighteen games in 1915, but most fans were even more intrigued by his powerful hitting. In the season opener, he lost 4–3 to the Yankees but hit his first major league home run. The homer off pitcher Jack Warhop delighted fans and amazed one reporter, who wrote that Ruth hit it "with no apparent effort."[28]

Boston beat Philadelphia four games to one in the World Series, but Ruth's only appearance was as a pinch hitter because Manager Bill Carrigan started only right-handed pitchers. In 1916 Ruth led Boston back to the fall classic with a 23–12 record that included nine shutouts, an American League (AL) record for left-handers that stood for more than fifty years.

After beating the Brooklyn Dodgers 2–1 in fourteen innings, Ruth joked to Carrigan, "I told you a year ago I could take care of those National League bums."[29] Boston won the Series in five games.

Hitting in Boston

In 1917 Ruth was 24–13 with a .325 batting average, but Boston failed to win the AL championship. In the 1918 season, which started late because the federal government limited the number of games due to World War I, Ruth had a 13–7 record and allowed opponents only 2.2 runs per game. But when Manager Ed Barrow put him in the outfield, Ruth's hitting began to overshadow his pitching.

Now making a princely $7,000, Ruth did not mind the extra duty because he loved to hit. When Ruth came to Boston, he had tried taking batting practice every day, something unusual for a pitcher and that irritated other players so much they sawed his bats in half. Since then Ruth had impressed everyone with his hitting. In 1915 he hit home runs in three consecutive games, a rare feat at the time; however, he only had one more that season.

When his at bats more than doubled in 1918 to 317, Ruth tied for the home run title with 11 but struck out a league-leading 58 times. The strikeouts were part of the new swing-for-the-fences style he was making popular. Other players quit trying to bunt or hit singles through the infield and were swinging as hard as they could to hit home runs.

Ruth starred in the 1918 World Series as Boston beat Chicago four out of six games. Ruth won the first game 1–0 and shut out the Cubs for seven innings in his second game before giving up two runs in a 3–2 victory. The sixteen innings gave Ruth a record streak of 29⅔ scoreless innings dating back to the previous World Series, a record unbroken for more than four decades. His daughter Julia Stevens said in 1997 that Ruth prided himself on his pitching: "With all those home runs and his great deeds as a hitter and outfielder, Daddy was probably proudest of his pitching. He never failed to talk about his pitching records. If somebody else didn't mention them, he would."[30]

Ruth Is Sold Again

The 1919 season was Ruth's last as a pitcher. Although still masterful with a 9–5 record, Boston put him in the outfield regularly and Ruth nearly tripled his 1918 total to a major league record of 29. The mark Ruth broke was set in 1884 by Ned Williamson of the NL Chicago White Stockings, a team known today as the Cubs.

Even though Ruth was an effective pitcher, Boston converted him into an outfielder after he began hitting so many home runs.

Williamson had hit an unprecedented 27 home runs, but only two on the road, because he played in Lakefront Park, a tiny stadium whose right- and left-field foul lines were more than a hundred feet shorter than average. To put Ruth's 29 homers into perspective, consider that no AL player had ever hit more than 16, Socks Seybold in 1902, and Gavvy Cravath led the NL in 1918 with only 8.

Ruth became a national sensation, and for the first time newspapers began running daily home run totals. But because Boston owner Harry Frazee was in financial trouble, he sold Ruth to the Yankees for a record $125,000 and a $350,000 loan so he could stage the play *No, No, Nannette*.

More Homers Than Ever

When Ruth's offensive barrage began to spark record attendance, owners approved rules for 1920 that would dramatically increase home runs and offense. Pitchers could no longer doctor the ball, and umpires began replacing scuffed-up balls with new ones. The season's offensive explosion was also aided by the A. J. Reach Company's new livelier ball. Major league teams in 1915 hit 384 home runs, a total that five years later jumped to 631, ten years later soared to 1,167, and in 1930 reached 1,565—four times as many home runs in just fifteen years!

Leading the way was Ruth, who nearly doubled his record to 54 and batted .376 in a season that transformed the nature of the game. Ruth's homers also boosted baseball's image, which had been tarnished by the 1919 "Black Sox" scandal.

Although the 1920 Yankees finished three games out of first place, Yankee owners Tillinghast Huston and Jacob Ruppert had gained the sports bargain of the century in Ruth, the key player in transforming a struggling team into baseball's greatest dynasty. Babe would lead the Yankees to seven league championships, the first in 1921 and the last in 1932, and four World Series titles.

Ruth had his finest season in 1921 when he bettered his home run record for the third straight year to 59 while setting career bests for average (.378) and 171 runs batted in (RBI). By the end of that season, the twenty-six-year-old Ruth already had 142 home runs to break the career record of 136 set by Roger Connor.

On September 30, 1927, when Ruth hit his 60th home run for a record that would stand for thirty-four years, he exultantly shouted in the clubhouse, "Sixty, count 'em, sixty. Let's see some other son of a bitch match that."[31]

The First Sports Superstar

Ruth was a perfect fit for glittering New York, where he won two more nicknames—"the Bambino" (Italian for "baby") and "Sultan of Swat"—while becoming the nation's most popular sports personality. New York sportswriter Richard Vidmer remembers:

> If you weren't around in those times, I don't think you could appreciate what a figure the Babe was. He was bigger than the president. One time we stopped at a little town in Illinois. It was about ten o'clock at night and raining

Ruth hits a home run in the stadium the Yankees were able to build in the Bronx, thanks to the huge crowds that Ruth attracted with his home runs.

[hard]. The train stopped for ten minutes. It couldn't have been a town of more than five thousand people, and by God, there were four thousand of them down there standing in the rain, just waiting to see the Babe.[32]

By 1921 Ruth was the game's highest paid player at $52,000. The Yankees increased their original offer of $50,000 when Ruth complained, "Well, there are fifty-two weeks in the year, and I've always wanted to make a grand a week."[33] Ruth would earn as much as $80,000, almost six times what other top players earned, but he was worth every dime. When Ruth arrived, the Yankees and NL New York Giants shared the Polo Grounds, a giant horseshoe-shaped stadium originally built as a polo field. But after Ruth's star quality in 1920 doubled Yankee attendance to nearly 1.3 million, the Giants were so embarrassed at being outdrawn in a stadium they owned that they told the Yankees to move.

New York's new stadium in the Bronx became known as "The House That Ruth Built," a sly reference to the fact that he was the reason the club had $2.5 million to finance it. In 1923 Ruth delighted an overflow crowd of more than 72,000 by smashing a home run in the first game played there.

In addition to his salary, Ruth made tens of thousands of dollars by endorsing products (everything from cigars to cereal), touring in vaudeville shows (one reviewer said Ruth had a nice singing voice), making movies, and playing postseason exhibition games.

The last venture landed him in trouble with Baseball Commissioner Kennesaw Mountain Landis, who in 1921 barred World Series players from exhibitions. When told about the ruling Ruth commented, "Tell the old guy to go jump in the lake."[34] But even newspapers that loved Ruth turned against him: "Baseball made Ruth, and not Ruth baseball," one paper wrote. "Baseball needs a Landis more than it needs a Ruth."[35]

Landis fined Ruth and two other Yankees $3,362, the amount of their World Series checks, and suspended them for the first six weeks of 1922. In his shortened season Ruth hit 35 home runs, four less than Ken Williams, and failed to win the AL title for the first time in four years. Ruth would win the title eight of the next nine years, the last time in 1931 when he and teammate Lou Gehrig tied with 46.

His Personal Life

The public was intrigued with Ruth because of his colorful lifestyle, including his gargantuan appetite. For breakfast Ruth might order eighteen eggs with steaks and chops, he could eat a gallon of ice cream, and one of his favorite snacks was several pounds of raw hamburger. In 1925 when Ruth became ill during spring training, reporters dubbed his health problem "The Belly-ache Heard Around the World." It was really an intestinal abscess that required surgery, but his fans *wanted* to believe the popular myth that Ruth became ill after gorging on hot dogs.

Bob Considine, who helped Ruth write his autobiography, said the Babe "thought every night was New Year's Eve."[36] Ruth loved to drink and party all night, and Yankee teammate Ping Bodie once joked, "I don't room with him. I room with his suitcase."[37] Ruth generally played well despite his carousing, but in one spring training game he was so groggy after a night of drinking that he crashed into a palm tree while chasing a fly ball.

In 1921 the childless Ruths adopted an infant, Dorothy, but their marriage even then was falling apart. Ruth was unfaithful to his wife throughout their marriage; he had girlfriends in every city his team played and also visited houses of prostitution. Helen left Ruth in 1926, but because they were Catholic they did not divorce, living apart until she died in a fire on January 11, 1929.

The final break in their marriage had been Ruth's first long-lasting romance, with Claire Merritt Hodgson, a former actress and showgirl he met in 1923. They were married in New York on April 17, 1929, the day the season opened. Ruth adopted her

31

daughter, Julia, and his new wife brought order to his life. Claire controlled their finances, writing Babe $50 checks for pocket money to limit his lavish spending, and they remained happily married until his death.

The Ruth Legend

Sportswriters like the *New York World*'s Heywood Broun flexed their creativity to turn Ruth into a mythical figure. After Ruth socked two home runs in a World Series game, Broun wrote, "The Ruth is mighty and shall prevail." Broun also whimsically commented, "We wonder whether new baseballs conversing

Ruth's affair with Claire Merritt Hodgson (pictured) contributed to the deterioration of his marriage to Helen Woodford.

in the original package ever remark: 'Join Ruth and see the world.'"[38]

But the facts were as fantastic as any tall tale. In 1926 Ruth befriended Johnny Sylvester, a young boy who was ill. Before the World Series that season against St. Louis, Ruth sent him a note saying, "I'll hit a home run for you in Wednesday's game."[39] Ruth did not hit just *one* home run for Sylvester, he hit *three* to fulfill his pledge.

His most mythical feat came on October 1, 1932, in a World Series game at Chicago's Wrigley Field. The Yankees had won the first two in New York and would sweep the Series in four games. When Ruth came to bat in the first inning, Cubs fans and players jeered and taunted the aging, potbellied slugger. They called him an "ape" and a "gorilla," slurs he had heard before because of his huge body and flat, thick-featured face. He quieted the insults with a three-run homer.

Ruth batted again in the fifth inning with the score tied 4–4. The first pitch was a strike, and when the Chicago players hooted loudly, Ruth turned and held up one finger. When Ruth took a second strike, he held up two fingers to the jeering players and said, "It only takes one to hit it."[40] The next pitch was a curve, and Ruth sent it scream-ing deep into the center bleachers to help the Yankees win 7–5.

Fact and myth quickly became intertwined in stories about the homer. Several writers wrote that Ruth "called his shot" by point-ing to the bleachers after the second strike. Although other ob-servers denied that, the facts never mattered to his fans, who *wanted* to believe Ruth had done it. "How the mob howled," Ruth said years later. "Me? I just laughed and laughed going around the bases, thinking about what a lucky bum I was."[41]

His Career Winds Down

The 1932 season was Ruth's last great one; he batted .341 with 41 home runs and 137 RBI and starred in the World Series. The Babe was getting old and heavy—one sportswriter said when Ruth ran the bases, he looked like "a balloon on toothpicks"[42]—and his numbers began to decline.

In 1933, at the age of thirty-eight, Ruth pitched one final time in the season's last game and hit his 34th home run, beating Boston. In 1933 he also hit the first home run in the inaugural All-Star Game, a two-run blast that gave the AL a 4–3 victory. After a 1934 season in which his hitting declined and he only had 22 home runs, Ruth toured the Far East and Europe. In Japan 60,000 people saw Ruth play in Tokyo and 80,000 in Osaka. The Babe was a hero wherever he went, but he returned home in February 1935 to find out the Yankees had released him.

Ruth had always said, "Don't quit until every base is uphill."[43] In 1935 it *was* uphill but because his pride had been stung, Ruth signed with the NL Boston Braves. Ruth was grossly overweight at 245 pounds and waddled more than ran, but he managed a home run in his first at bat.

By May 12 Ruth realized he had made a mistake and wanted to retire, but the Braves asked him to play for a few more weeks to boost attendance, the real reason they signed him. Ruth continued to play, and on May 25 hit three home runs against Pittsburgh. The last was 550 feet, the second longest in major league history. Only Yankee great Mickey Mantle's 565-foot homer in 1953 is be-lieved to have been longer.

When Ruth played his last game on May 30 in Philadelphia, a career that began with a strikeout on July 11, 1914, ended with a weak ground ball for an out. In 2,503 regular season games over twenty-two years, Ruth averaged .342, hit 714 home runs, and drove in 2,211 runs. As a pitcher Ruth also had a sparkling 94–46 pitching record.

His Last Years

When his playing days were over, Ruth wanted to manage but no team wanted him. Baseball executives believed Ruth, who had often argued with umpires and his own managers, was too undisciplined and that he was too dumb; his memory was so bad that Ruth called almost everyone he knew, even friends and teammates, "Doc" or "Kid," pronouncing the latter "keed." But sportswriter Fred Lieb denies Ruth was stupid:

> I refute stories that make him such a numbskull. Though his language invariably was colored with vulgarity and profanity, he often made intelligent comments on New York City and its politics, the Yankees, visiting players, and the chances of the other fifteen major league clubs [to win a pennant]. Once when Ruth and I were guests of the Gehrigs at their home, I was surprised to overhear Ruth speaking German to mom Gehrig.[44]

In retirement Ruth was saddened at his rejection by baseball and missed the limelight. As his wife Claire remembers: "Babe

Suffering from a rare form of cancer, Ruth walks on the field of Yankee Stadium for the last time and receives a standing ovation from the crowd.

would often sit by the phone, waiting for the call [for a job in baseball] that never came. Sometimes when he couldn't take it any longer, he'd break down, put his head in his hands, and weep."[45]

But baseball didn't forget Ruth entirely. On June 12, 1939, Ruth was among the first group of players inducted into the Baseball Hall of Fame; and after he was diagnosed with cancer in November 1946, baseball officials decided to honor him before he died. On April 27, 1947, with nearly 60,000 fans cheering him at Yankee Stadium, Ruth made a speech that was broadcast around the world. "There's been so many nice things said about me, I'm glad I had the opportunity to thank everybody. Thank you,"[46] he told the adoring crowd. He was also honored that day in other major league parks.

Suffering from a rare cancer that affected his nose and mouth, Ruth received an experimental combination of radiation and chemotherapy treatment. His condition improved and although terribly weakened, Ruth returned to Yankee Stadium one last time on June 13, 1948, for the ballpark's twenty-fifth anniversary. Using a bat as a cane, his once mighty body shrunken by disease, Ruth hobbled onto the field to a final standing ovation. The Yankees honored him by retiring his uniform number: 3.

The greatest baseball player there ever was died on August 16, 1948, in New York at age fifty-three. When his casket was placed in Yankee Stadium, more than 100,000 people filed by to say good-bye to the Home Run King. And more than fifty years later, in 1999, a panel of experts assembled by The Associated Press news service honored the Babe yet again by voting him the greatest baseball player of the last one hundred years, as well as the Athlete of the Century. His feats had proven grand enough to eclipse even sports legends like Michael Jordan, Jim Thorpe, Muhammad Ali, Wayne Gretzky, and Jim Brown, who held the next five spots behind Ruth in balloting to honor the twentieth century's greatest sports stars.

CHAPTER 3

Roger Maris: Battling the Legend of the Babe

When Roger Maris surpassed Babe Ruth with his 61st home run on October 1, 1961, he should have been thrilled to accomplish what so many great ballplayers had failed to do for thirty-four years. Instead, the twenty-seven-year-old blond, crewcut slugger for the New York Yankees felt only relief that a long, grim ordeal was over. "As a ballplayer," Maris said wearily, "I would be delighted to do it again. [But] as an individual, I doubt if I could possibly go through it again."[47]

Throughout his season-long chase of baseball's most cherished record, Maris battled not only opposing pitchers, but hostile fans who felt Maris was unworthy to replace the Home Run King, a media horde that dogged his every step, and the legend of the Babe. When Ruth died in 1948, famed sportswriter Grantland Rice composed an epiclike poem that ended:

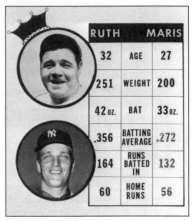

RUTH		MARIS
32	AGE	27
251	WEIGHT	200
42 oz.	BAT	33 oz.
.356	BATTING AVERAGE	.272
164	RUNS BATTED IN	132
60	HOME RUNS	56

Many fans thought Maris was unworthy of replacing Babe Ruth as the Home Run King.

> The Big Guy's left us with the night to face,
> And there is no one who can take his place.[48]

Rice's prophecy came true in 1961 as fans refused to accept Maris as Ruth's rightful heir. Ironically his record homer was hit in Yankee Stadium, still lovingly called "The House That Ruth Built" more than a quarter century after the Babe quit playing.

Roger Eugene Maras

Maris was born Roger Eugene Maras in Hibbing, Minnesota, on September 10, 1934, the second son of Rudy Maras Sr. and Connie Sturbitz Maras. He changed his name in 1955 because minor league players were ribbing him about it, pronouncing it "Mareass." When Maris altered the spelling, his whole family did.

Unlike Ruth, he was part of a loving, close-knit family and grew up in the relative innocence of small-town America. When Roger was five his father, a mechanic for the Great Northern Railroad, was promoted to supervisor and the Marases moved to Grand Forks, North Dakota. Five years later they moved to Fargo, North Dakota.

The elder Maras had been a fine athlete and so were his two sons. Roger and Rudy Jr., fifteen months older, played many sports including ice hockey, their father's favorite game. In Grand Forks they lived in an apartment and the boys worked odd jobs because money was tight. Maris's uncle Jerry March remembers his hardworking nephew as a young boy:

> I still have in mind the picture of Roger when the Empire Builder train came through Grand Forks during the dinner hour. He had newspapers and magazines under his arms ready for sale. But he was so small that he didn't know how to make change. When people gave him money, he would just pull out a handful of coins and hold it out. He looked so confused people usually let him keep the change.[49]

A High School Star

Although they were talented, the Maras boys did not become sports stars until they deserted Fargo Central High School for Bishop Shanley High School. "Bud and I would be responsible for splitting the town in half when we switched schools," Maris once said. "The people in Fargo never forgave me."[50] The brothers left Central because they did not like the football coach and did not get much playing time. After missing a year of competition due to the switch, Rudy, a senior, and Roger, a junior, became multisport stars in the 1950–51 season. In football Roger caught two touchdown passes from Rudy in a dramatic victory over Fargo Central, and in basketball Bishop Shanley beat Central twice, with Rudy the high scorer in both games.

Maris was such a fine running back that he was offered a scholarship to the University of Oklahoma, one of the nation's powerhouses in football. But Maris chose baseball, a sport he had not always loved as much as Rudy:

> It was my brother who forced me to play baseball and I mean *forced* me. If he went to play, he dragged me along. If he found me sitting around the house, he grabbed me by

the ear and pulled me out. If I had been bigger I might have put up an argument. But I didn't catch up to him [in size] until we were in high school, and by that time nobody had to force me to play.[51]

The Maras boys played American Legion baseball, and by his senior year Roger, six feet tall and 190 pounds, was a powerful hitter. When Roger graduated in 1953, he received a $5,000 bonus to sign with the Cleveland Indians. Tragically that same year Rudy, who also wanted to play professionally, was stricken with polio. The illness destroyed his dream.

Minor League Years

At his request, the Indians assigned Maris to begin his minor league career on May 1 for Fargo-Morehead, a team in the Class C Northern League. Maris quickly worked his way up through the minor leagues, which have several levels based on the ability of its players. As players improve, they are promoted to higher leagues, which are designated by letters in ascending order to Triple-A, the level just below the major leagues.

Maris was successful from his first game at Barnett Field in his hometown of Fargo, hitting .352 in 114 games with 9 home runs and 80 RBI to become the league's Rookie of the Year. In 1954 he hit .325 with 32 home runs in the Class B Three-Eye League in Keokuk, Iowa; and in 1956 with the Triple-A Indianapolis Indians, he batted .293 with 17 home runs and 75 RBI.

In 1956 Maris married Pat Carvell, his high school sweetheart. Unlike Babe Ruth, he would remain faithful to her. Pat described their date for the senior prom:

> Roger came dressed in a suit because hardly anyone could afford to rent a tuxedo. He borrowed his dad's beat-up 1932 Chevrolet and came up the steps with that nervous half-smile of his, self-conscious. In his right hand there was a box with a corsage. Roger was always very considerate. That's one of the first things I noticed about him.[52]

A Major Leaguer

Maris opened the 1957 season with the Cleveland Indians. In the season opener on April 16, he stroked three singles and in the next series hit the first of his 275 career home runs, a grand slam that helped the Indians beat the Detroit Tigers 8–3. Maris was hitting well until he broke two ribs on May 10 in a collision at home plate while trying to score. He slumped after the injury, batting .235 for the season with 14 home runs and 51 RBI.

Although Maris had a solid rookie season, he angered Cleveland by refusing to play winter ball in the Dominican Republic to refine his skills. His first child, Susan, had been born while Maris was on the road with the Indians, and he wanted to be with his family. That winter he sold advertising and did a sports show for a Fargo radio station.

After fifty-one games in 1958, the Indians traded Maris and two other players to the Kansas City Royals. It was in Kansas City, Royals manager Harry Craft explains, that Maris became a home run hitter:

> Roger learned to hit the ball in the air in Kansas City. That's what a hitter needs to hit home runs. He had a good quick stroke, good actions at the plate and good concentration. He didn't hit tape measure jobs the way [Mickey] Mantle was doing then, but he hit hard line drives and they got in there. That was all that counted.[53]

Weakened in May by an emergency appendectomy, Maris hit only 16 homers in 1959 but raised his average to .273. He showed so much promise that the Yankees acquired him on December 11 in a six-player trade. Maris, who heard of the trade while listening to the radio at home in Raytown, Missouri, was unhappy about going to New York. But legendary manager Casey Stengel was delighted: "I got this new man and I expect him to hit some long balls for me."[54]

"Julie" and Maris

When Maris visited New York for the first time after being traded, he was picked up at the airport by Julius Isaacson, a fan who often helped new players. They became good friends even though the newest Yankee surprised "Julie":

> Suddenly, I see this kid who looks lost. It had to be Maris because of the crew cut. But what an outfit: sweater, corduroy jeans, and white buckskin shoes. I told him he can't dress like that with the Yankees and Roger said, "The hell with them. If they don't like the way I look or dress, I won't play for them. I can go back to Kansas City."[55]

Maris's comment explains a lot about his personality. A small-town boy who never reveled in New York's glitter as Ruth had, Maris felt uncomfortable in 1961 when the media spotlight became

Maris, shown at home with his family, sometimes felt lonely during his first season with the Yankees because his wife and children could not be with him.

focused on him. Maris was stubborn and angered easily, always did things his way, and was quick to defend his position on any issue. But when Isaacson helped him adjust to New York, these two men from very different backgrounds—an athletic country boy and a Jewish big-city businessman—became close friends. And friendship meant as much to Maris as family.

Although sometimes lonely because his wife and children—Susan, Roger Jr., and Kevin (sons Randy and Rich and daughter Sandra were born later)—remained at their home in Raytown, Maris had a terrific season. He hit .283 with 39 home runs and 112 RBI to win the league's Most Valuable Player award along with a Gold Glove for defense. And although New York lost the World Series to the Pittsburgh Pirates in seven games, Maris socked two home runs in the fall classic.

An Untouchable Record

As the years passed after Ruth's 60–home run season, more and more players determined to be the next Sultan of Swat had begun swinging for the fences; in 1959 the major league home run total exceeded two thousand for the first time. A few sluggers came close, but nobody could top the Babe. In 1930 Hack Wilson of the

Chicago Cubs hit 56 home runs, two years later Jimmie Foxx of the Philadelphia Athletics had 58, and in 1938 Hank Greenberg of the Detroit Tigers tallied 58.

Greenberg, Cleveland's general manager when Maris signed, believes so many great players had failed to break the record that by 1961 "everybody seemed to accept it wouldn't happen. It was like Ted Williams hitting .406 or Joe DiMaggio hitting in 56 straight games [records set in 1941 that were still intact after the 1999 season]."[56]

Maris was first compared to Ruth in 1960 when he hit 25 home runs in less than half a season before slowing down the rest of the year. Even after his hot start, Maris predicted the record would never be broken.

The M&M Boys

In 1961 Maris did not get his first home run until April 26. "Ten games had gone by and I hadn't hit one," Maris remembers. "I began to wonder if I would ever hit one."[57] In mid-May Maris was still batting an anemic .210 with only 4 home runs, and the Yankees were struggling with a 16–14 record. It was around this time that Yankees' president Dan Topping told Maris to relax. "Don't worry about your batting average," he said. "Shoot for the fences. We'll pay you on the basis of home runs and RBI."[58]

At ease after the vote of confidence, Maris hit his 5th homer on May 19 off Pete Burnside of the Washington Senators, clubbed homers in his next two games, and finished May with an even dozen. In June Maris slammed 15 more to help New York win twenty-three of thirty-three games.

The remarkable thing was that teammate Mickey Mantle was also slugging at a Ruthian pace. An outfielder who in 1956 hit 52 home runs and was one of the game's biggest stars, Mantle matched Maris homer for homer. Mantle finished June two home runs behind Maris with 25, the same number Ruth had on that date in 1927.

By then sportswriters were calling them the "M&M Boys," and the media frenzy about Ruth's record had begun. By mid-July when the first of that year's two All-Star Games was played, the controversy had also begun.

A Record and an Asterisk

The addition of two new teams forced the American League to expand its 1961 schedule to 162 games, eight more than Ruth played, which led Baseball Commissioner Ford Frick to question

During the 1961 season, teammates Roger Maris and Mickey Mantle (left) were both on pace to make a run at Ruth's home run record.

whether Ruth's record would really be broken if it took a player more than 154 games to surpass it. Frick, however, was biased, as a close friend of Ruth's who for years had been paid to ghostwrite articles under Ruth's name.

When Maris and Mantle were both ahead of Ruth's 1927 pace at the All-Star break on July 17 with 35 and 33 home runs respectively, the commissioner ruled that unless a player broke it by the season's 154th game, an asterisk would accompany the batter's name in the record books. Although Maris argued that a season was a season no matter how many games were played, he hated the controversy:

> That was a debate I wanted no part of. I wasn't even thinking about the record. I was just trying to see what I could do and hoping to do the best I could. The Commissioner made the ruling, and there was nothing I could do about it. I was just playing ball, doing the best I could, and hoping for a pennant.[59]

The Media Spotlight

The Frick ruling intensified the media storm swirling around Maris. In Ruth's era newspaper writers rarely interviewed players and there were no television and radio reporters. But Maris, playing in the nation's media center, was hounded daily by reporters about the home run chase. Former catcher Tim McCarver, once a teammate of Maris and now a top television analyst, remembers how the introverted Maris struggled under the constant media pressure:

> That he was trying to go one up on the immortal Babe Ruth, in New York yet, was the worst thing that could have happened to him. He was as ill suited to play in the media capital as Mickey Mantle was in the 1950s after he arrived from Commerce, Oklahoma. Quite simply, Maris, too, became a victim of culture shock.[60]

Although Mantle was also shy at first, his outgoing personality endeared him to the media. Maris was comfortable with reporters he knew well but uncooperative with strangers, and when stories appeared that seemed to be based more on fiction than fact, he became defensive and withdrawn.

Maris became tired of answering the same questions over and over, and some queries even made him angry. When Maris passed up a chance at a homer on August 7 by bunting against Los Angeles, reporters refused to believe him when he said he was happy because it helped New York win: "If there is anything I can't stand, it is to try to answer honestly a question and explain exactly how I feel, then have someone act as if I were kidding them and start laughing at me."[61] Years later Maury Allen of the *New York Post*, who wrote about the Yankees in 1961, admitted, "I do feel ashamed of us sometimes."[62]

What bothered and bewildered Maris the most were media claims that he and Mantle were bitterly jealous, stories written even though they were sharing an apartment with teammate Bob Cerv. Mantle said they joked about the alleged hostility:

> Through it all we remained close. There was never any jealousy. I rooted for him and definitely rooted for myself. If there was a rivalry it was a friendly one. In fact, when we did hear some rumor about us not getting along, we used it as a running gag. Like, we'd sit in the apartment, reading the paper. I'd put mine down, look over at him, and say, "I hate your guts." He laughed. Some feud.[63]

Although there was no personal animosity between them, Maris believed fans and Yankee executives were rooting for the more popular Mantle to inherit Ruth's crown. "I don't think the Yankees wanted me to break Ruth's record. They favored Mickey to break it,"[64] he said years later.

And there were *always* questions about Ruth, the legend who haunted him throughout 1961. Many people began writing him letters, some filled with obscenities that claimed he was a "bum" who was lucky to hit so many home runs and that he was unworthy of taking Ruth's record. It was an attitude shared by some members of the media, and even Ruth's widow complained, "I hope he doesn't do it. Babe loved that record above all."[65]

Fed up with letters and comments that he was not good enough to surpass Ruth, Maris finally lashed out at writers:

> Don't ask me about that record! I don't want to talk about it. One guy wrote that I don't deserve to break the Babe's record. Now I admire Ruth. He was the greatest but what am I supposed to do, stop hitting homers? They make it sound as if I'd be committing a sin if I broke the record.[66]

Motivated by Scorn

In a game in Washington after the All-Star break, Mantle hit three home runs to go ahead of Maris 36–35. But in a doubleheader at Yankee Stadium on July 25 against Chicago, Maris homered four times to lead 40–38. His big day in the season's ninety-sixth game put him seven ahead of Ruth's pace and pushed the record quest to a new level of intensity.

Manager Ralph Houk was criticized for favoring Maris by batting him third ahead of Mantle, which gave Maris more at bats late in games. Houk simply responded that the batting order was the best for his club and refused to change it. Maris, however, was able to use all the negative remarks to his advantage:

> Actually, I believe the one thing which really drove me toward the record and which kept me battling when the whole thing got out of hand was all the people who had been knocking me. I was tired of hearing and reading that I was a lousy hitter, that I wasn't in Ruth's class and didn't deserve to have so many homers. I just felt I'd like to break the record just to hear them squeal louder.[67]

A New Home Run King

On September 1, the date in 1927 when Ruth had 43 home runs, Maris was at 51 and Mantle at 48. By this time Maris was under so much strain that patches of his blond crewcut began falling out. "I'm going nuts, Mick. I can't stand much more of this," he told Mantle, who replied, "You'll just have to learn to take it, Rog, there's no escape."[68]

People under extreme pressure sometimes say stupid things and Maris was no exception. He criticized fans who booed him or shouted obscenities, said the record would make his family financially secure, and attacked the media. Some of his statements were taken out of context, but even Maris admitted some of his comments were dumb.

Part of his anxiety was the need to surpass Ruth in 154 games. When Maris did not get his 59th homer until September 20, the 155th game, some of the pressure eased. Maris no longer cared if his record would be sullied by an asterisk and no longer worried about Mantle, who missed the final games of the season with a hip injury to finish with 54 home runs.

Maris hit number 60 at home on September 26 off Baltimore's Jack Fisher. To the amazement of millions of people, Maris then took a day off because he was exhausted. He traded in one of his

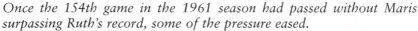

Once the 154th game in the 1961 season had passed without Maris surpassing Ruth's record, some of the pressure eased.

final chances at surpassing Ruth so he could relax by going shopping and having a leisurely dinner with his wife.

That left a final three-game series at home against Boston, Ruth's old team. Maris was hitless on Friday and managed only a single on Saturday. Before Sunday's 162nd and final game, Maris sat quietly at his locker, puffing on a cigarette while Pat, as she had all season, prayed to Saint Jude, the Catholic Church's patron saint of lost causes.

In the first inning, Maris hit a weak fly ball for an out off six foot five right-hander Tracy Stallard. The crowd booed Stallard in the second inning when his first two pitches were balls; they feared he would walk Maris. At 2:43 P.M. Stallard threw a fastball, low but across the plate. Maris swung mightily and sent the ball in a towering arc 380 feet into the right-field stands. When it landed near the spot where Ruth hit his 60th home run on September 30, 1927, a dazed Maris rounded the bases: "I saw it was a good fastball. I was ready and I connected. As soon as I hit it, I knew it was number 61. Then I heard the tremendous roar of the crowd. I could see them all standing. Then my mind went blank. I couldn't even think as I went around the bases. I was in a fog."[69]

Among the accolades that poured in was a telegram from President John F. Kennedy that said, "The American people will always admire a man who overcomes great pressure to achieve an outstanding goal."[70] Maris helped the Yankees win the World Series against Cincinnati, and his game-winning home run in the ninth inning of the third game, with the series tied 1–1, was the key hit in the series.

Bitter Aftermath

In 1962 Maris sought a pay raise from $42,000 to $100,000. When he only received $72,500 plus $5,000 in living expenses, a sum smaller than the $80,000 Ruth earned three decades earlier and less than Mantle's $100,000, Maris became bitter toward the Yankees. In its own way the 1962 season was even more difficult than 1961 as Maris slumped to 33 home runs and 100 RBI. Mantle remembers how brutally fans treated Maris: "In 1962 the fans gave him the worst beating any ballplayer ever took. From April straight through September they stayed on his back. I guess they expected him to hit 62 home runs. They weren't satisfied with 33. So they booed him in every ballpark."[71]

His deteriorating relations with the media created more problems for Maris. Miffed that Maris stood him up for an interview during spring training, New York sportswriter Jimmy Cannon wrote that success had spoiled Maris, whom he nicknamed the "whiner" and labeled "a man of treacherous smallness."[72]

Maris, bothered the next season by a hand injury he said the Yankees failed to properly treat, never hit more than 26 home runs again and in 1966 was traded to the St. Louis Cardinals after hitting only 13 homers. He played two more years, helping the Cardinals win the 1967 World Series over Boston, and hit his last home run on September 15, 1968.

His Final Years

When Maris retired the next year, he and Rudy started a beer distributorship in Gainesville, Florida. Embittered by his experience in baseball, Maris stayed away from the game until April 12, 1978, when he consented to appear at Yankee Stadium for an Old-Timers day. A huge standing ovation that day helped heal some of his old wounds. "It's like obituaries," Maris joked. "When you die they always give you good reviews." But Maris was touched, admitting, "I didn't get the goose pimples for nothing. It was nice."[73]

The obituaries were also kind when Maris died on December 15, 1985, after a long bout with cancer, the same disease that took Ruth. He was buried in Fargo in a service attended by Mantle and other Yankee greats.

CHAPTER 4

Hank Aaron: Breaking a Record and Defeating Bigotry

Hank Aaron knows the truth of the proverb "Time heals all wounds." It took Aaron almost a quarter century to exorcise the anger, hurt, and bitterness that poisoned his quest to break Babe Ruth's career home run record.

Like Roger Maris, Aaron discovered the ghost of Ruth to be a foe formidable as any pitcher as he neared 714 home runs. Even though Aaron said at the time, "I don't want them to forget Ruth, I just want them to remember me,"[74] some people were so angry he was going to dethrone Ruth that they sent him hate mail, telephoned death threats to ballparks where he played, and shouted obscene taunts during games. And all because of the color of this African American's skin. "Dear Super Spook," began one venomous letter.

Hank Aaron's quest to break Ruth's career home run record was plagued by racism.

"You are pretty damn repugnant to break the Babe's [record]."[75]

But on April 8, 1999, when a capacity crowd of 47,225 gathered at Turner Field in Atlanta to mark the twenty-fifth anniversary of his record, Aaron admitted he had finally made peace with his record: "I'm enjoying it, very much so now. Twenty-five years ago I was a very bitter person. I've aged and taken my

48

mother's advice: don't worry about things I don't have control over."[76]

Growing Up in Segregated Alabama

Henry Louis Aaron was born in Mobile, Alabama, on February 5, 1934, the day before Ruth's thirty-ninth birthday, to Herbert and Estella Aaron. They had moved to Alabama's only seaport from Camden, a rural community north of Mobile, in search of a better way of life than picking cotton. His father worked as a boiler-maker's assistant in the shipyards and the family rented a home for $6 a month.

The Aarons lived in Down the Bay until 1942 when they moved to Toulminville, another African American community where his father built a home from scrap lumber on land he had scrimped and saved to purchase. The house had only six rooms, no windows, and an outdoor bathroom, but the couple and their eight children rejoiced in it. "We were a proud family," Hank Aaron remembers, "because the way we saw it, the only people who owned their own homes were rich folks and Aarons."[77]

Even though Herbert worked and Estella sometimes cleaned homes, money was so tight that the Aaron children also had to find jobs. Hank mowed lawns, picked potatoes, delivered twenty-four-pound blocks of ice, and sold soft drinks from the back of a flatbed truck to spectators at baseball games. He had to make his own baseballs by wrapping rags or nylon hose around old golf balls because he could not afford to buy a real one. When there was no ball, Hank and other kids took turns throwing and hitting bottle caps with a broomstick.

Becoming a Baseball Player

In 1948 his life changed when the Brooklyn Dodgers came to Mobile for an exhibition game. Aaron wrote how special it was to see Jackie Robinson, who in a game on April 15, 1947, against the Boston Braves became the twentieth century's first African American major league player:

> The day Jackie Robinson came to town, I skipped [school] to hear him speak in the auditorium on Davis Avenue. That same day, I told my father that I would be in the big leagues before Jackie retired. Jackie had that effect on all of us—he gave us our dreams. He breathed baseball into the black community. Before then, whenever I said I wanted to be a

Jackie Robinson, the twentieth century's first African American major league ballplayer, was an inspiration to Aaron.

ballplayer, daddy would set me straight. He said, "Ain't no colored ballplayers." But he never said that anymore after we sat in the colored section of Hartwell Field and watched Jackie Robinson.[78]

Aaron became good at baseball and at age sixteen was playing for the semiprofessional Mobile Black Bears for $3 a game—home games only because his mom said he was too young to travel.

The Indianapolis Clowns

In 1952 the eighteen-year-old Aaron began his professional career in the Negro Leagues with the Indianapolis Clowns. Although his family believed deeply in education, Aaron left school three weeks before finishing his final semester in high school; the lure of $200 a month was too much for a poor teenager to resist. In 1957 when Aaron won the National League's Most Valuable Player award, he reminisced about leaving home to join the Clowns:

"Most valuable player," I said out loud. Not bad for a kid who left home with two dollars in his pocket, two pairs of pants and two sandwiches in a brown paper bag. My mother cried and my sisters cried, and I thought back to that day at the railroad station in Mobile, a little black kid taking his first train ride to be a baseball player at the age of eighteen. My mother made me take the sandwiches. "They may not serve you on the train, son," she said. "You take these sandwiches. I don't want you going hungry."[79]

In the Negro Leagues, a bus was the team's hotel as well as a means of transportation. "We didn't have roommates, we had seatmates,"[80] Aaron once joked. Players slept on the bus most nights while traveling between cities to play as many as ten games each week. Since many restaurants would not serve them because of their skin color, the players ate on the bus after buying food from small country stores.

Five years after Robinson broke baseball's color barrier, only eight of the sixteen major league teams had African American players. But every club was now scouting the Negro Leagues, and Aaron quickly captured the attention of the Milwaukee Braves by hitting over .400. When talent scout Dewey Griggs saw Aaron get seven hits in nine at bats in a May 25 doubleheader, he noticed something strange: Aaron was batting cross-handed, his left hand placed incorrectly above his right.

Between games Griggs asked the right-hander to bat the correct way by switching his hands, and Aaron's first time up using the correct style he hit a home run. Remembers Aaron:

> I was never taught any other way. I didn't play in Little League. I grew up in Mobile, where everything [like that] was forbidden to black people. I had a bat. I picked it up, and I thought I was doing the right thing. I played in the Negro leagues holding the bat that way, but I couldn't have reached the majors batting that way.[81]

Griggs's report was so glowing that a few days later the Braves outbid the Dodgers for Aaron, buying his contract for $7,500 and offering him $350 a month, $100 more than the Dodgers. On June 11 he reported to Milwaukee's minor league club in Eau Claire, Wisconsin.

Eau Claire, Wisconsin

Even though the Eau Claire Bears of the Class C Northern League had two other African American players, Aaron went into culture shock: he had never been around so many white people or competed against white players. Aaron dealt with it easily on the field, but soon discovered that learning to live in a white world was more difficult:

> It was not a hateful place for a black person—nothing like the South—but we didn't exactly blend in. The only other black man in town was a fellow who used to stand on the street corner flipping a silver dollar. Wherever I went, I had the feeling that people were watching me, looking at me as though I were some kind of strange creature. There was nothing in my experience that prepared me for white people.[82]

Although he played well, Aaron was so miserable after a few weeks that he packed his clothes and called home to say he was quitting. His mother said that was fine, but older brother Herbert Jr. bawled him out: "Man, are you out of your mind? Don't make a fool out of yourself. Henry, don't make a mistake."[83] Luckily, Aaron took his brother's advice and stayed because eighteen days later he was named the starting shortstop in the league's All-Star Game.

Aaron hit .336 with 9 home runs and 61 RBI to be named Class C Rookie of the Year. After the season he rejoined the Clowns and helped them win the Negro League World Series, hitting 5 home runs and batting over .400 in thirteen games. He also returned home and finished work for his high school degree.

Racism in the Minor Leagues

In 1953 the Braves promoted Aaron to their Jacksonville, Florida, Class A team in the South Atlantic (Sally) League. With that honor, however, came the unenviable task of integrating minor league baseball in southern states like Florida, Georgia, and Alabama. Aaron and African American teammates Horace Garner and Felix Mantilla had to endure racial taunts from fans *and* white players without becoming angry. They knew that if they caused an incident, it might hurt the continued integration of major league baseball. The meanest fans, ironically, were in Aaron's home state of Alabama:

> [Montgomery] was about the only town where we got "nigger" thrown at us. I thought they'd get used to us after a while, that they'd settle down and get off our backs, but it lasted the whole season. Strangely enough, Montgomery was the only town where black players were put up in a

hotel. In all the other towns, we stayed in private homes [segregation barred them from the hotels and restaurants that accepted their white teammates].[84]

African American players triumphed by showing southern whites they could play well and act honorably despite the difficult, hostile situation; one reporter for the *Jacksonville Journal* even wrote that Aaron helped start the city down the road to racial understanding. Aaron batted .362 with 22 home runs, both of which led the league, and drove in 125 runs to win the Most Valuable Player award.

That spring Aaron also met Barbara Lucas, who was attending business school in her native Jacksonville. They were married on October 6.

The Milwaukee Braves

After learning to play the outfield in the winter Puerto Rican League, Aaron reported to spring training in 1954 hoping to make the Braves' major league roster. He got his chance because of his ability and an unfortunate accident to Bobby Thomson, who broke his ankle in an exhibition game on March 13. The next day Manager Charlie Grimm walked over to Aaron in the dugout, picked up Aaron's glove, handed it to him, and told the young player he was now the club's starting left fielder.

Aaron quickly showed he had the talent to replace Thomson, who was famous for his dramatic home run that won the 1951 National League pennant for the New York Giants. Hitless in his first regular season game, on April 15 against Cincinnati Aaron collected his first major league hit, a double, and eight days later in St. Louis hit his first home run. Although his season ended September 5 when he broke his ankle while sliding, he hit a respectable .280 with 13 home runs and 69 RBI.

In their first four seasons in Milwaukee, the Braves, who had left Boston in 1953 because of declining attendance, were the first team each year to draw one million fans, and in 1957 they set a major league record with more than 2.2 million fans. Aaron, along with pitchers Warren Spahn and Lew Burdette, shortstop Johnny Logan, and third baseman Eddie Mathews, made the Braves one of baseball's best teams.

Aaron helped Milwaukee win the 1957 National League pennant, batting .322 with 44 home runs and 132 RBI to win the league's MVP award. He led the NL in home runs for the first time by matching his jersey number of 44, a total he would reach three more times in his career.

An ankle injury to Bobby Thomson (left) enabled Aaron to get his first playing experience in the major leagues.

Now known as "Hammerin' Hank," Aaron hit a dramatic home run to clinch the NL pennant. On September 23 with team-mate Logan on base in the eleventh inning, he smashed a curve ball four hundred feet into the centerfield bleachers at County Stadium to beat St. Louis 4–2. The sellout crowd of nearly 41,000 fans went wild, and his teammates celebrated by carrying Aaron off the field. In a nostalgic return to County Stadium in 1999, Aaron said: "The greatest thrill I ever had, bar none, was that year we clinched the pennant when I hit the home run off Billy Muf-fett. That, to me, was probably the greatest thing that ever hap-pened to me as a baseball player."[85]

His 109th career homer put Milwaukee into the World Series against the New York Yankees. Burdette won three games, but the twenty-three-year-old Aaron hit three home runs and batted .393 to win MVP honors in a series the Braves won four games to three.

Racism Even for a Hero

The day after Aaron hit his pennant-winning homer, his picture was on the front page of the *Milwaukee Journal*. Next to it was a photo from Little Rock, Arkansas, where whites had rioted against African American students integrating a high school. That fall Aaron discovered that not even being a World Series hero made him safe from such racism. Invited to speak to a service club in Mobile, Aaron asked to bring his father. "The man just hemmed and hawed, and finally he said they just couldn't allow it. It was one thing for a black World Series hero to speak to their club, but it was another thing to have his black daddy sitting with all the good white men in the audience,"[86] Aaron recalls. He canceled the speech.

Although they were now allowed to play baseball, African American players still faced discrimination. On February 27, 1958, when Aaron and Felix Mantilla were driving to spring training, they were run off the road in Florida by white youths jealous that the players were traveling in a new car. The Braves told Aaron not to mention the incident to reporters, but he did. "I was beginning to lose my timidity and speak up about the racism in baseball,"[87] he explains.

In 1958 African American players rented rooms for spring training in a home in Bradenton, Florida, because local hotels and restaurants would not accept them. The problem was not solved until 1960 when Aaron demanded the club fix the problem. But for several more years after that, African American players still had trouble finding places to sleep and eat in major league cities like Cincinnati, Ohio, and St. Louis, Missouri.

From Milwaukee to Atlanta

In 1958 the Braves lost the World Series to the Yankees. The next year Milwaukee won fifteen of its last twenty games to tie the Dodgers in the regular season, but then lost to them in a playoff series. Although Aaron kept slugging home runs, the Braves went downhill, sliding in the standings and in attendance. "Players came and went like livestock,"[88] Aaron says of those years in which the Braves self-destructed.

As they had done when moving from Boston to Milwaukee, the Braves in 1966 fled to Atlanta in search of greater attendance and revenue. In his first game that season, Aaron hit two home runs to reach 400 for his career and on April 29 smashed his seventh of the season and first in Atlanta.

Realizing that Fulton County Stadium was an easier ballpark to hit home runs in than Milwaukee County Stadium, Aaron changed his batting style so he could hit to left field consistently with more power. The result was that in 1966 he led the NL with 44 home runs and 127 RBI. Aaron kept hitting home runs at a fierce pace and on July 14, 1968, in Atlanta became only the eighth player to reach 500 for his career.

People now began to wonder if the thirty-four-year-old could break Ruth's record.

Chasing the Babe

Several months before Ruth died in 1948 he predicted, "Somebody will break my record of 60 homers in a season. No one will ever come close to my lifetime 714 homers."[89] But in 1969 Aaron hit 44 and in the next few seasons bashed 38, 47 (his career high), 34, and 40 to total 713 home runs heading into 1974. Aaron had slugged his way to the edge of greatness by being a steady if unspectacular player, one often overshadowed by more charismatic stars like Mickey Mantle and Willie Mays.

Aaron, who in 1970 also got his 3,000th hit, said the key to his success was patience: "Patience—which is really the art of waiting—is something you pick up pretty naturally when you grow up black in Alabama. When you wait all your life for respect and equality and a seat in the front of the bus, it's nothing to wait a little while for a slider inside."[90]

By 1970 the home run chase was consuming his life. That season his marriage began falling apart and the Aarons divorced in 1971, a season in which Aaron hit 47 home runs. "I threw myself into baseball," he said, "to get my mind off [his personal life]. The kids [Gail, Hank Jr., Lary, Dorinda, and Ceci] were always on my mind. There were times when I'd really be depressed."[91]

It was also in 1971 that he met Billye Williams, who interviewed him on her Atlanta morning television show. They were married on November 12, 1973, and she brought stability back to his life as he headed into the final stretch of his run for the record.

Breaking the Record

In 1974 Eddie Mathews, his teammate in Milwaukee, became his manager. In his first at bat of the season, Aaron hit number 714 off Jack Billingham on April 4 in Cincinnati to tie Ruth. Mathews held him out of the next game and wanted to do the same thing the next day to make sure Aaron set the record in Atlanta, but Baseball Commissioner Bowie Kuhn ruled Aaron had to play.

His marriage to Billye Williams (pictured with Aaron) brought stability back to Aaron's life.

When Aaron failed to hit a homer, a press corps numbering over three hundred accompanied the club to Atlanta for its April 8 home opener. The pressure on Aaron was tremendous, not only from the media and its constant questions about Ruth, but because of the racist letters he was receiving. But when Aaron had mentioned the mail to sportswriters the previous May in Philadelphia, he was deluged with positive letters: in 1973 he received over 930,000 letters, more mail than anyone that year, even the president, and most were positive.

The long ordeal ended on April 8 at 9:07 P.M. when he hit a sinker from Al Downing of the Los Angeles Dodgers over the left field wall for his 715th career home run. As he circled the bases, Aaron was in a delightful fog, happy and relieved his quest was over:

> I don't remember the noise or the two kids that I'm told [came onto the field and] ran the bases with me. My teammates at home plate, I remember seeing them. I remember my mother out there, and she hugging me. That's what I'll remember more than anything about that home run when I think back on it. I don't know where she came from, but she was there.[92]

Back to Milwaukee

His skills eroding with age, Aaron in 1974 batted .268 with 20 home runs and 69 RBI. When the season ended, he went to Japan for a home run contest against Sadaharu Oh, who totaled 868 home runs in his career in Japan. After beating Oh 10–9, Aaron received a telephone call that night at 3 A.M. from Allan "Bud" Selig, the principal owner of the Brewers, telling him he had been traded to Milwaukee.

Aaron was happy even though he candidly told Selig, "You're not getting the same player that left Milwaukee. I have a slower bat, I don't hit as many home runs as I used to."[93] That was fine with Selig, who knew that even an aging Home Run King would be a powerful drawing card for the American League franchise he had worked so hard to get to replace the Braves.

Although Aaron batted only .234 with a dozen home runs, in May he broke Ruth's RBI record of 2,211 in a game against the Detroit Tigers. Surprisingly, that record received little attention from fans or the media. In two years as a Brewer, Aaron hit only 22 home runs and his final homer came on July 20, 1976, off Dick Drago in Milwaukee.

Aaron is mobbed by teammates after hitting his record-breaking home run.

His seasons with the Brewers were a lackluster finish to a brilliant career. But when Aaron returned to Milwaukee on July 20, 1999, on the twenty-third anniversary of his final home run, he said it had been "a tremendous thrill for me to finish my career where it started."[94] In a pregame ceremony, Selig, who in 1998 became the first owner to be elected baseball commissioner, called Aaron "the greatest player of his generation."[95]

1999—A Great Year for Aaron

The visit was part of baseball's year-long tribute to Aaron, who in retirement was not ignored like Ruth—he has been an executive with the Braves since he quit playing—but who never felt his accomplishments were appreciated as much as they should have been. "He was bitter," admits longtime friend Bob Allen, who worked in public relations for the Milwaukee Braves. "He never thought he got the recognition he deserved. He told me one time, 'I guess I'm going to have to wait until I die before they realize how good I really was.'"[96]

However, many feel that Aaron never became as popular as stars like Mantle and Mays because he lacked their vibrant personalities and flair for the dramatic. Even he once admitted, "I wouldn't pay to see Hank Aaron. I wasn't flashy."[97]

Aaron also felt slighted that Bowie Kuhn did not attend the game in which he broke Ruth's record and that in 1982 nine of 415 baseball writers did not vote to elect him to the Hall of Fame; neither Aaron, nor many others, could comprehend how any writer could have failed to think he belonged in the Hall of Fame.

But in 1999 with close friend Selig now commissioner, baseball acted to heal any existing breach. The celebration started on February 5 in Atlanta with a gala sixty-fifth birthday party that raised $1 million for Aaron's Chasing the Dream Foundation, which provides educational opportunities for underprivileged children.

Selig announced the new Hank Aaron Award, which will be presented annually to hitters in each league with the most combined hits, home runs, and RBI. The award is a fitting tribute for a player who averaged .305 for twenty-three seasons and holds records for most home runs, most RBI (2,297), most extra-base hits (1,477), most total bases (6,856), and is third in hits (3,771) behind only Pete Rose and Ty Cobb.

And Aaron had finally come to terms with Ruth, the legend he once chased. "If I ever met Babe Ruth and had to ask him one question," he said, "I would ask him if he was proud of me. And I think he would answer, 'Yes, yes, I'm very proud of you.'"[98]

CHAPTER 5

Mark McGwire: Chasing Roger and the Babe

When Mark McGwire hit 70 home runs in 1998, he not only awed sports fans with prodigiously long home runs, he touched them with his love for his son, Matthew, displaying a heart even bigger than his massive weight-lifter forearms. "I tell him almost every day I talk to him that what I do in the game of baseball, I do for him,"[99] explains McGwire. After homering on September 8 to surpass Roger Maris, McGwire stomped on home plate and joyously lifted his ten-year-old son high above him. "What a wonderful feeling for a father,"[100] said the new Home Run King.

Mark McGwire's imposing stature earned him the nickname of "Tree" in middle school.

The fatherly devotion was nothing new. In 1987 when Mc-Gwire hit a major league rookie record of 49 home runs for Oakland, he skipped the A's final game to witness Matthew's birth. Many were amazed he gave up a chance at the milestone of 50 homers, but McGwire knew what was *really* important. "You always have another chance to hit 50," he said, "but you'll never have a chance to have your first child again."[101]

It would be nine more seasons before McGwire topped that magic mark—1996 when he hit 52. When McGwire blasted 58 in 1997, comparisons with the legendary Babe Ruth that were planted when he was a rookie reached full bloom. But the ghost of Ruth, which so cruelly haunted Maris and Hank Aaron, failed to daunt the six foot five, 250-pound "Big Mac," who said, "I really believe he's up there watching."[102]

If the Babe was a spectator in a heavenly box seat, he witnessed the most remarkable home run race ever.

A Happy Youth

Mark David McGwire was linked with Maris from birth. Born in Pomona, California, on October 1, 1963, two years to the day after Maris hit his 61st home run, McGwire hit his 62nd two days before what would have been Maris's sixty-fourth birthday.

McGwire grew up in a middle-class family in Claremont, California, one of five sons of John and Ginger McGwire. His nickname at La Puerta Middle School was "Tree" because he was so big, not surprising considering his dad and brothers are all at least six feet three inches tall and weigh at least 220 pounds. The McGwire boys were star athletes, and Dan, the tallest at six foot eight, became a National Football League quarterback.

When Mark began caddying for his dad at age five, golf was the first game he played. McGwire took up other sports, and when he started Little League baseball at age ten, he hit a home run in his first at bat. "I swung and closed my eyes and it went out,"[103] McGwire remembers. Although he became a star, his father did not want him to become egotistical: "As parents we never gloated over Mark's success. Even when some of the city's old-time ballplayers and opposing coaches would stop and tell me Mark was a future big leaguer, I never let him know about it."[104]

Like Ruth, McGwire was a pitcher; and like Maris, he played American Legion baseball, once pitching a no-hitter in the championship game of a tournament in Wyoming. As a senior at Damien High School in 1981, McGwire batted .359 with 5 home runs to go with his 5–3 pitching record and stingy 1.90 earned run average (ERA).

McGwire had a good fastball, nearly ninety miles per hour, and the University of Southern California (USC) offered him a scholarship at the same time as the Montreal Expos selected him in the June player draft. When Montreal offered only an $8,500 signing bonus, he decided to attend college.

From Pitcher to Hitter

In the spring of 1982, McGwire was 4–4 with a 3.04 ERA while hitting .200 with 3 home runs. It was then his life was changed forever by Ron Vaughn, an assistant coach who thought McGwire's future, like Ruth's, was as a hitter. Vaughn asked him to devote himself to hitting while playing for the Anchorage Glacier Pilots in the Alaska Summer League.

In Alaska, McGwire was lonely being so far away from his parents, brothers, and girlfriend, Kathy Hughes, a USC batgirl. Like a young Aaron miserable in the minor leagues in Eau Claire, Wisconsin, he became homesick and wanted to quit. But McGwire stayed, worked hard, and under Vaughn's guidance batted .403 with 13 home runs.

Randy Robertson, a childhood friend and his USC roommate, said McGwire returned wanting to play every day. "He dedicated himself to hitting [and getting stronger]," recalls Robertson. "He'd sit on the couch in front of the TV in his boxer shorts doing curls with weights."[105]

USC coach Rod Dedeaux fought the switch but used McGwire as a pitcher only seven times because he hit so many home runs. He hit a school record of 19 homers and the next year hammered 32, as many as any USC player ever hit for an entire *career.*

Two years after his summer in Alaska, Oakland selected him tenth in the June draft. Two years later McGwire hit his first major league home run.

The Minors

McGwire played in the 1984 Olympics before reporting to Oakland. Although it was one of the great experiences of his life, the United States lost the gold medal game to Japan 6–3. In sixteen minor league games in Modesto, California, McGwire hit .200 with 1 home run, a poor start attributed to fatigue from a college season followed by the physical and emotional grind of the Olympics.

In 1985 Oakland converted McGwire to a third baseman, and he hit .274 with 24 home runs to be named California League

Rookie of the Year. McGwire began 1986 in Double-A at Huntsville, Alabama, but played only fifty-five games before being elevated to Triple-A Tacoma, Washington.

After hitting .318 in seventy-eight games with 13 home runs, the A's called him up to the major leagues; but in his debut on August 22, McGwire failed to get a hit in a 3–2 loss. Fittingly for someone who would surpass Ruth and Maris, the game was in Yankee Stadium; the first thing McGwire did at the ballpark was to view plaques dedicated to the two great hitters. McGwire got his first major league hit in his third game and his first home run the next night off Walt Terrell.

In eighteen games McGwire hit .189 with 3 home runs and 9 RBI, a quiet debut for a player who a year later would become a home run hero.

Rookie Sensation

Converted to a first baseman because he made too many errors at third, McGwire started slowly, finishing April with 4 home runs. But in early May he hit 5 in a three-game series and in one sixteen-game stretch banged 11 to finish May with 15, one less than the record for the month that Mickey Mantle had set in 1956.

With the speed of one of the balls he was rocketing out of American League ballparks, McGwire became a star, played in his first All-Star Game, and earned the nickname "Big Mac," which he preferred over other whimsical suggestions such as "Orange Crush" (for his red hair), "Agent Orange," and "Marco Solo." McGwire finished July with 37 home runs and on August 14 broke the major league rookie record with his 39th.

But he discovered it was easier to hit homers than deal with the media. In June the *Los Angeles Times* first coupled the words *McGwire, Ruth,* and *Maris* in one headline, and media pressure intensified because he had a chance of overtaking Maris. McGwire, who complained that reporters were constantly pestering him with questions, blamed the media for hurting his concentration and causing an August slump. Baseball analyst Tim McCarver believes the media has hurt many hitters chasing the record: "The media isn't supposed to be part of the story, but invariably [until 1998] the player's home run outputs went down as the number of relentless reporters around them increased. Potential challengers have been worn down by the media."[106]

McGwire led the AL with 49 home runs and batted .289 with 118 RBI to win Rookie of the Year honors. The year before teammate Jose Canseco had 33 homers to win the award, and when he hit 31 more in 1987, the media dubbed the powerful duo the "Bash

Brothers." They would lead Oakland to the World Series each of the next three years.

Problems—On the Field and Off

Success, however, proved a mixed blessing. In 1988 when McGwire had only 16 home runs at midseason, reporters and fans began asking what was wrong. "They expect me to have 33 homers at the All-Star break," he griped. "Give me a break."[107] McGwire finished with 32 homers, 99 RBI, and a .260 average—solid numbers but down from a year earlier. In the third game of the World Series, a 2–1 victory over the Los Angeles Dodgers, McGwire hit a ninth-inning home run. But it was his only hit in seventeen at bats and Oakland's only victory.

One reason McGwire struggled was that his personal life had disintegrated. He married Kathy in December 1984 but they divorced a year after celebrating Matthew's birth. McGwire claims they married too young and did not know what love was all about. But Kathy believes "women, fame, [and] glamour" broke them up; even McGwire admits, "I did so much stupid stuff."[108]

Oakland's prolific home run hitters Jose Canseco (far left) and McGwire (second from right) were dubbed the "Bash Brothers."

McGwire remained on good terms with his ex-wife, who gained custody of Matthew.

The next two seasons McGwire hit 33 and 39 home runs and Oakland returned to the Series, beating San Francisco but losing to Cincinnati. In 1990 when McGwire was the first player to hit more than 30 homers in each of his first four seasons, the A's nearly tripled his salary to $1.5 million. But not even money could make McGwire happy, and in 1991 he bottomed out as a player and a person.

The A's were struggling, fans were taunting him for not helping the club enough (his average had dropped to a career low of .201 with only 22 home runs and 75 RBI), and he was going through a painful breakup with a girlfriend. After the season's final game, McGwire searched his soul:

> I was at a crossroads in my life. I remember driving home [to Los Angeles]. I knew I had five hours by myself to think. I didn't turn the radio on, didn't play any music, nothing. I just thought. I was so down. I thought about everything my father had been through. I mean, he never even got a chance to play baseball [he had polio as a child]. I thought about how much I really loved the game, and I decided there wasn't any room for pouting or complaining or anything but doing my best.[109]

A therapist helped him come to terms with his life and realize how important his son was. "We talk all the time," McGwire says of Matthew. "We talk about everything. If there's one thing I've learned, you have to talk."[110]

McGwire rededicated himself, lifting weights to add twenty pounds of muscle, studying pitchers, and doing exercises to improve his abysmally weak (20-500) eyesight. In 1992 McGwire, now sporting his trademark goatee, smashed 42 home runs and might have won his second home run title if a muscle strain had not sidelined him for twenty games. But McGwire hit only 9 each of the next two seasons as injuries to his left heel limited him to twenty-seven games in 1993 and forty-seven in 1994.

The 1995 season started late because of the players' strike the previous August, but McGwire, healthy again, hit 39 home runs and drove in 90 runs for a team that finished fourth. The best was yet to come.

Closing in on the Record

After tearing muscle tissue in his right foot during spring training in 1996, McGwire was so disheartened he almost quit. The media was also questioning whether he had become injury prone from too much weight lifting; he now had twenty-inch biceps and a 17½-inch neck. "I was very, very depressed," McGwire admits. "My parents and friends talked me out of [retirement]. Thank God."[111] He returned in late April and by mid-June had 25 home runs. On September 14 McGwire finally reached the 50 mark with home runs in both games of a doubleheader and finished the season with 52.

McGwire started fast in 1997 with 11 homers in April and 34 by July 16. But he hit only five in July when he felt turmoil about the possibility of being traded. Finally traded on July 31 to the St. Louis Cardinals for three minor league pitchers, McGwire's slump continued while he adjusted to National League pitchers; he hit only one home run in the first ten days of August. Despite the slump, he finished tantalizingly close to the record with 58.

On September 16 the Cardinals signed him to a three-year $28.5 million contract. At a news conference he promised to donate $1 million a year to his Mark McGwire Foundation, which helps physically and sexually abused children. "Let's just say children have a special place in my heart,"[112] he said, and that night sealed the deal with a 517-foot homer.

Happy with his new club, McGwire was ready to make history.

A Fast Start

McGwire smashed a grand slam home run in the March 31, 1998, opener to beat Los Angeles 6–0 and hit balls out in each of his next three games: in their record-breaking years, Ruth did not homer until April 15, 1927, and Maris not until April 26, 1961. McGwire also unveiled a new home run celebration—instead of bashing forearms with teammates after reaching home plate, he delivered high fives with a closed fist followed by an exaggerated punch to the gut of the next batter.

On April 14 after hitting 3 homers in a 15–5 win in St. Louis over the Arizona Diamondbacks, McGwire commented on how happy he was that Matthew was on hand as a batboy (a privilege written into McGwire's contract): "The first year I played in the big leagues Reggie Jackson told me that he always regretted that he didn't have a child to watch him hit his 500 home runs. I just feel fortunate that he is around to see me. That makes it special."[113] Matthew became his lucky charm. His first appearance led to 3 homers; and after McGwire failed to hit one for several games, Matthew kissed his bat on July 11 and he smashed his 38th.

McGwire has said that having his son, Matthew, at the games as a batboy makes his baseball experience special.

On April 30 McGwire hit his 11th home run to tie for the major league lead with Vinnie Castilla of the Colorado Rockies and Ken Griffey Jr. of the Seattle Mariners, who in 1997 hit 56. His 13th on May 8 put him one behind Griffey and was the 400th of his career, a milestone he reached faster than any player in history. "I've had adversity in my personal life and in my professional life. I'm a perfect example," McGwire said, "of a person who can conquer things if they can dream and believe in themselves."[114]

Eight days later in a 5–4 victory over the Florida Marlins, McGwire smashed a pitch 545 feet to tie Griffey at 16. McGwire has three of the ten longest home runs in history—the longest was Mantle's 565-footer in 1953—and like Ruth, part of the awe McGwire inspires is how far his home runs travel. His homers are so high and so long that they are called "moonshots" and he is so powerful he scares pitchers. "He's the one guy in baseball," claims Philadelphia's Curt Schilling, "who could hit a ball that goes in one side of you and out the other, and it would be going just as fast when it came out."[115]

In the next nine days, McGwire hit 9 more to take control of the race and end the month with 27, the most anyone ever had through May. The media was going wild, but McGwire believed it was too early, saying the record was not a legitimate topic until somebody had 50 by September.

His complaint fell on deaf ears.

The Media Onslaught

Maris had nearly gone crazy dealing with only fifteen to thirty writers, but the media was now far larger and more complex. In addition to newspaper and magazine writers, there were local, national, and international radio and television reporters, sometimes even writers for Internet publications. "It's totally out of hand. I feel like a caged animal,"[116] McGwire said on June 18 after hitting number 33.

When daily media sessions began to overwhelm McGwire, the Cardinals issued guidelines restricting media access (something the Yankees should have done for Maris in 1961). On July 20 before the first game of a series in San Diego, California, McGwire was surrounded by cameras and thirty reporters in the one interview he now held to start every road trip. Leaning nonchalantly against a locker, McGwire's exasperation was evident:

> I don't play the game for this. I'm sick of seeing my mug. The media sets this up like it's going to happen. . . . I assume people want this record to be broken. So let's use some sense. Why not wait until somebody gets close to breaking the record? If people want to see something done, it makes sense to do this in a way that won't wear the person down.[117]

His only negative coverage appeared in late August when everyone from sportswriters to political pundits reported, commented, and philosophized about his use of androstenedione, a testosterone-producing pill he had taken for a year to help his workouts. Although banned in football and the Olympics, the drug was legal in baseball and McGwire had never tried to hide his use; the story broke when a reporter noticed a bottle of the pills in his locker. The controversy upset McGwire, who believed he had done nothing wrong.

Luckily for McGwire, another player was now sharing the spotlight. While McGwire had left behind early competitors like Griffey, Sammy Sosa of the Chicago Cubs came from nowhere to challenge him by hitting a major league record of 20 home runs in June.

Mark and Sammy

Fans were intrigued by contrasts between the two. Sosa grew up in poverty in the Dominican Republic instead of middle-class affluence in California, had a personality that was far more joyous and open than McGwire's gruff stoicism, and was black instead of white. Yet during their remarkable season, the two players forged a heartwarming friendship that brought out the best in both.

On May 30 Sosa had 13 home runs to McGwire's 27, but his phenomenal June tied him with Griffey at 33 and pulled him within four of McGwire, at 37. When Sosa hit two on August 10 in an 8–7 win over San Francisco to tie at 46, he downplayed his chance of beating McGwire. "I still believe he's 'the Man.' No matter what happens, he's 'the Man,'"[118] said Sosa.

To add spice to the race, the Cardinals and Cubs, bitter rivals for more than a century, went head to head dramatically several times in the final two months. On August 19 in Chicago's Wrigley Field, Sosa took the lead with his 48th home run in the fifth inning. But fifty-eight minutes later McGwire connected to tie Sosa and the game and in the tenth inning hit his 49th to win the game 8–6.

The only other lead Sosa held would come on September 25 when he hit number 66 against Houston, but McGwire matched him forty-five minutes later with one off Montreal's Shayne Bennett. The six foot, 200 pound Cub spurred McGwire to greatness and even helped him learn to enjoy the historic season. Explains McGwire:

> In early August, guys on other teams came up to me and said, "Hey, just relax. Enjoy the ride." I sat back and thought about it and said, "These guys are right." It just so happened that we got together right around the time I was starting to enjoy it. I changed my mind, and then Sammy was there. He made me think even more, "Hey, this is fun. This is a game we love to play."[119]

McGwire homered twice on August 20 to reach 51, putting him three ahead and making him the first player to hit 50 in three straight seasons. When they both had 55 heading into September, interest rocketed to new heights. Even batting practice became an event, especially after McGwire hit one ball so hard it did $10,000 worth of damage to a scoreboard. "They're showing batting practice on TV," said an incredulous McGwire. "Now that's psycho."[120]

McGwire homered twice against Florida on September 1 to reach 57 and surpass the sixty-eight-year-old NL record of 56 set by the Cubs' Hack Wilson. McGwire hit two more against the Marlins the next day and on September 5 became the third to reach 60 when he belted one off Cincinnati's Dennis Reyes, accomplishing the feat in twelve fewer games than Ruth (154).

Maris was in his sights as Chicago came to St. Louis for a historic series.

The Record

On September 7 McGwire gave his father a unique present on his sixty-first birthday. The night before when they had dinner, his dad had challenged him by saying, "I got to 61, so [you] should be able to do it, too."[121] McGwire's 430-foot first-inning solo homer off Mike Morgan tied the record, and he did it in 144 games, eighteen fewer than Maris.

The next night in the fourth inning, McGwire, who earlier had lovingly cradled the bat Maris used to hit his 61st, smashed a low but powerful line drive off Steve Trachsel 341 feet to left for his

After hitting his record-breaking home run, McGwire displayed his respect for Roger Maris by hugging members of the late slugger's family, including his son Richard Maris (pictured).

shortest homer of the season. Almost forgetting to touch first, McGwire trotted around the bases in a daze while cameras flashed and 50,000 fans erupted in joy:

> I was in shock, I was numb. *I did it!* I had all these things running through my mind, and I was just floating in outer space. I can't even remember everything I did. I do remember I saw Matthew and I saw my teammates, and all of a sudden I was just standing there acknowledging the crowd when I glanced over and saw the Maris family. I just took off to their box and hugged them and told them that their father was in my heart. I hadn't planned it. It just happened. I knew what they were going through and the feelings they were feeling.[122]

It was also a special moment for the Maris family because McGwire honored their father, who in 1961 had been reviled by some and ignored by others. "I couldn't be happier," said Roger Maris Jr. "He would have been very proud of Mark as a player, but I think more so as a person."[123]

Although Sosa came in from the outfield to hug McGwire, he wasn't ready to concede the home run title. The Cubs' star tied him at 62 before McGwire came out of his post-record daze on September 15 to smash number 63. They would be tied three more times including at 66 going into the season's last weekend.

In the final series against Montreal, McGwire homered twice in each of the last two games. The record 70th was a 370-foot, game-winning, three-run home run off rookie Carl Pavano to break a 3–3 tie. McGwire's homers in 1998 traveled a total of 29,598 feet, an incredible 5.6 miles!

McGwire finished the 1998 season with 70 home runs, although pitchers walked him 162 times.

In April, 70 home runs had seemed an impossible number, like running the mile in three minutes or lifting a thousand pounds. Amazingly, McGwire almost had 71. After hitting his 65th in Milwaukee on September 20, McGwire bashed a ball into the bleachers later in the game that was ruled a ground rule double by umpire Bob Davidson because a fan allegedly interfered by reaching over the outfield railing to catch it; television replays showed it should have been ruled a homer. McGwire lost many other opportunities to pad the record by drawing an NL record of 162 walks, often to the accompaniment of boos from fans who wanted to see him hit one out.

When the long grind was over, even McGwire admitted, "I'm like in awe of myself right now."[124] But when asked how he wants to be remembered, McGwire humbly responded, "that I was a good father. And, oh, by the way, he was a pretty good ballplayer."[125]

CHAPTER 6

Sammy Sosa: Happy with 66!

Just hours before Mark McGwire would tie Roger Maris with his 61st home run, Sammy Sosa broke up both Big Mac and the gigantic media corps assembled for their historic confrontation by coyly announcing, "I have to say, bezbol been berry, berry good to me."[126] First mouthed two decades earlier on *Saturday Night Live* by comic Garrett Morris in the role of Chico Esquela, a Hispanic player turned sportscaster, the line borders on racial stereotype because of Esquela's difficulty pronouncing words like "baseball" and "very"—a problem Sosa definitely does *not* have. But Sosa,

Sosa's cheerful demeanor helped to alleviate the stress caused by the chase for the home run record.

who high-fived a laughing McGwire after tossing out the surprise line, uttered the words with such warmth and good humor that he captured everyone's heart.

The phrase became a Sosa trademark for two reasons. First Sosa, who grew up in the Dominican Republican, is an example of someone born to bitter poverty who used his talent to create a rich new life through baseball. Second, the fact that he could make a self-deprecating joke during the most dramatic home run duel in history symbolized the joy with which Sosa embraced the challenge of battling McGwire for the title of Home Run King.

Sosa finished four home runs short of McGwire's record 70. But the former shoeshine boy, once so poor he had to fashion baseball gloves from discarded milk cartons, still surpassed Maris by five and the immortal Babe Ruth by six. Fans were also touched that at the height of the race, Sosa took time to aid his homeland after it was hit hard in September by Hurricane Georges.

Growing Up in Poverty

Samuel Sosa was born on November 12, 1968, to Bautista and Lucrecia Montero in San Pedro de Macoris, a city of about 125,000 in the Caribbean Sea on the island of Hispaniola, which the Dominican Republic shares with the Republic of Haiti. Although his mother did her best, Sammy, brothers Luis, Juan, and Jose, and sisters Raquel and Sonia grew up bitterly poor after their father died when Sammy was seven.

The family name was changed to Sosa when Lucrecia remarried. They were still poor, the children sleeping on the floor in a tiny two-bedroom apartment without indoor plumbing. Lucrecia cooked meals for factory workers and the children worked to make ends meet. By age seven Sosa was shining shoes in the Parque Duarte, a tree-lined square in the center of town, selling oranges for a dime, and washing cars.

Some of his customers were baseball stars like Pedro Guerrero and Joaquin Andujar. "Those players when they came home, I saw they had everything. They were like kings. I always said I wanted to be like that,"[127] Sosa remembers. Another customer was Bill Chase, a Massachusetts native who opened a shoe factory in San Pedro de Macoris in 1979 and would become a father figure to the young boy. Chase remembers their first meeting:

> The first night in town I go down to the town square, there are two hundred kids shining shoes. They [Juan and Sammy]

shined my shoes. Every night, I'd go to the square and just watch everybody, and the kids shined my shoes. Sammy had that big smile. They were likable kids. They knew how to get to your heart.[128]

Chase started paying the brothers to do odd jobs at his factory—a fringe benefit was being able to shower there—and Chase and his wife, Debbie, began buying members of the Sosa family clothes and other necessities. Juan and Sammy shined shoes for people visiting Chase's factory, sometimes receiving $5, a huge sum in that poor country.

Becoming a Ballplayer

Sosa never played much baseball until he was fourteen because he went to school half-days and worked. "My brother [Luis] said, 'Come on, I'm going to put you in the league because you're going to be the one who can make it happen.' And from there, it just happened,"[129] Sosa recalled, a scenario reminiscent of the relationship between Roger and Rudy Maris. After Chase bought him a $100 baseball glove in 1981, Sosa began developing into a good player.

Because the Dominican Republic had produced major league stars like Ozzie Virgil, Juan Marichal, and Felipe Alou, baseball scouts were always searching there for new talent. In 1985 Sosa came to their attention. Sosa was sixteen years old, five feet ten inches tall, and a skinny 150 pounds, but in a tryout his raw skill impressed Texas Rangers scouts enough to win a contract.

When Sosa received a $3,500 signing bonus on July 30, 1985, he gave almost all of it to his mother. "For the Dominican, our family comes first," Sosa says. "[Players are] always going to go back home to take care of 'my mother, my father, my cousin, my aunt'—everybody."[130] His one extravagance, like Ruth, was to buy his first bicycle.

Minor Leaguer

The last thing Sosa saw before leaving his homeland in 1986 was his mother, crying over his good fortune and his departure. Sosa hit .275 for Sarasota (Florida) in the Gulf Coast Rookie League, but life was difficult in a new, strange land. Unable to speak English, when Sosa went out to eat he would either point to a picture on the menu or order what everyone else was having. Fortunately, some teammates helped him adapt to the new culture: "I got lucky because there were some Puerto Rican players who I hung out with. They helped me a lot. This is the way that

I was able to understand life here in the United States. After I had the opportunity to get past that transition, everything became easier."[131]

Sosa rose rapidly in the minor leagues, and the Rangers promoted him to the majors early in 1989. In his major league debut on June 16 against the New York Yankees (the team that McGwire played his first game against and that Ruth and Maris played for), Sosa had two hits in four at bats. Sosa hit his first home run on June 21 off hard-throwing Roger Clemens, but after slumping he was demoted on July 20 to Triple-A Oklahoma City.

Nine days later Sosa was traded to the Chicago White Sox and on August 23 played against the Minnesota Twins, rapping out three hits including a home run. His love affair with Chicago had begun.

Chicago White Sox Years

In 1990 in his first full season in the major leagues, Sosa averaged .233 with 15 home runs and 70 RBI while stealing 32 bases. But Sosa also struck out 150 times and his overall game lacked polish. "I became a professional ball player with a lot of talent and no discipline at home plate because I didn't have time to play when I was a boy,"[132] Sosa admits.

A high number of strikeouts in succeeding years seemed to indicate Sosa cared more about hitting for power than a high average, which might have helped his team more. But as Latin American baseball scout Omar Minaya points out, "You've got to understand about Latin players when they're young—or really any players from low economic backgrounds. They know the only way to make money is by putting up big offensive numbers."[133]

Sosa became a fan favorite along with other young players like Frank Thomas and Robin Ventura as they helped the Sox post a 94–68 record. Sosa started strong in 1991 with 2 home runs and 5 RBI in the season opener against Baltimore, but after struggling early he was demoted in late July. He spent a month in the minor leagues before being recalled in August and finishing the year with Chicago.

Sosa batted only .203 with 10 home runs and 33 RBI in 116 games for the White Sox. But the cross-town rival Chicago Cubs saw something they liked and on March 30, 1992, traded George Bell for Sosa and pitcher Ken Patterson.

A Chicago Cub

In 1992 Sosa played only sixty-seven games because of two injuries, a broken bone in his hand and a fractured ankle, but the next year finally unleashed his star potential when he hit .263 with 33 home runs and 93 RBI. He also stole 36 bases to become the Cub's first player to steal 30 bases and hit 30 home runs, a significant achievement indicating a rare blend of speed and power in one player.

Sosa, however, was still considered a selfish player who cared more about personal statistics than team victories. After his 30-30 season, some people in baseball complained that no player had ever been more excited about a year in which his team finished in fourth place. Sosa added to this negative image by showing up at spring training in 1993 wearing a huge diamond-encrusted necklace with the numbers "30-30," an affectation that seemed to verify his vanity. The necklace, however, was just part of his fondness at the time for flashy clothes, fast cars, and nightlife. "I used to be kind of wild,"[134] he once admitted. Sosa spent money lavishly on himself and his family and went through a brief, stormy first marriage, but he settled down after wedding Sonia Esther in November 1991 and became a devoted family man.

Sosa's second wife, Sonia Esther, helped him to settle down and become a devoted family man.

A dancer on a Dominican television show, Sonia admits she was unimpressed when they first met at a disco. "I didn't know he was a ballplayer. I thought he was just another traveling salesman in gold chains,"[135] she said. But they kept seeing one another, fell in love, and were married. They have four children—Keysha, Kenia, Sammy Jr., and Michael.

1997—A Miserable Season

Although Sosa played well in the next few years and never hit less than 25 home runs, the Cubs were perennial losers. In 1995 when Jim Riggleman became Chicago's third manager since Sosa was acquired, he showed his new maturity by telling Riggleman he would do whatever it took to win. "He came to me one time and said, 'Hey, anything you want me to do, just tell me. Just talk to me man to man,'"[136] Riggleman recalls.

Sosa started strong that season, was chosen for his first All-Star team, and had 36 homers and 119 RBI, but the Cubs finished only two games above .500 (73–71) in a season shortened by the players' strike. It was also the year Sosa began to flirt with home run history. He hit his 100th career homer on May 14 and the 10,000th homer in Cubs history on August 14; on May 21 his thirteenth-inning homer gave Chicago its 9,000th franchise victory.

In 1996 Sosa was having a brilliant season with 40 home runs, 100 RBI, and a .273 batting average until a pitch thrown by Florida's Mark Hutton on August 21 broke his right hand. Disappointed that his fine season ended prematurely, Sosa had a tough time being sidelined by injury. "When I was hurt, I was like a kid. I'd go there, watch the games and do nothing. I hope that never happens to me again."[137]

In 1997 both Sosa and the Cubs got off to a miserable start. Chicago lost a club record fourteen straight games to open the season and finished a dismal 68–94. But Sosa had worked hard to improve his fielding, and although he hit .251 with 36 home runs and 119 RBI, his season was blemished by a club record of 174 strikeouts, the most in the National League.

In an ironic quirk of timing, on June 27 Chicago signed Sosa to a four-year contract worth $42.5 million that made him the third highest paid player in baseball at the time. Coming during another losing season, the contract proved to be both good and bad. Although Sosa said it helped him "relax and be more patient"[138] because it gave him security, he admitted people began expecting too much from him. The expensive contract was criticized by fans and the media, but Cubs president Andrew B. MacPhail defended it. "Obviously," he said, "we're banking on how much we respect Sammy as an individual. We believe he will continue to work hard and mature and improve."[139]

In 1998 the Cubs' trust in Sosa would return huge dividends.

Sammy's Amazing June

Sosa had fame, personal success, and financial security, but he had never experienced the thrill of a World Series. The talented player dubbed by some "Sammy So-So" because he had never led his team to the playoffs came to spring training in 1998 with a new attitude: "I said to myself, 'I have to come back and be ready for 1998 and do what I have to do. I have to sacrifice myself and be a better contact guy.' We weren't all together last year. That has to change this year. Everybody has to play for each other. I'm here to win a championship."[140]

Several coaches have helped Sosa improve his hitting, including Billy Williams, the former Cub star and Hall of Famer. During the off-season Sosa worked hard to learn a new style suggested by hitting coach Jeff Pentland, who sent him videos of several hitters to help him refine his swing. "We needed to come up with some way for him to read and recognize pitches sooner," said Pentland, "and that way we'd be able to slow him down."[141]

In April Sosa slammed only six home runs and in May just seven, but he was hitting for a higher average and driving in more runs. The Cubs were also winning with new players like fellow Dominican Henry Rodriguez, Mickey Morandini, reliever Rod Beck, and rookie pitcher Kerry Wood, who on May 6 tied a major league record by striking out twenty batters.

At the end of May Sosa was fourteen behind McGwire and not considered a threat to break the record. But when Sosa returned on June 1 after several days off due to a wrist injury, he hit 2 home runs in the Cubs' tenth straight victory to begin the most fantastic home run month in history. After his 19th homer of the season on June 7 in a 13–7 win over the White Sox, he joked about his new power: "I'm practicing by playing Nintendo baseball with my daughter and my wife. They usually beat me, so I have to take it out on other teams."[142]

The homers kept coming, including three on June 15 against the Milwaukee Brewers' Cal Eldred and a pair on both June 19 and June 20 against Philadelphia to give him 29. Suddenly Sosa had powered his way into the home run race and was the talk of baseball.

On June 25 Sosa smashed his 19th June homer to break the major league single-month record set by Detroit's Rudy York in 1937. The record blast came in Tiger Stadium, where York had played, but any joy over his 32nd homer was dimmed by a 6–4 loss. "I'm happy I'm in the book, but for me it don't mean nothing because we lost the game,"[143] Sosa complained.

Sosa hit one more on June 30 to push the one-month record to 20, tie Ken Griffey Jr. of the Seattle Mariners for second place with 33, and pull within four of McGwire.

The Mac and Sammy Show

Although Griffey stayed close into August, the contest was now strictly between Sosa and McGwire. And the fans loved "The Mac and Sammy Show." Although McGwire was becoming testy over the unrelenting media attention that had plagued him since spring training, it was new and exciting for Sosa to be treated like a superstar.

Unlike many athletes suddenly thrust into the spotlight, Sosa weathered the media storm, continuing to be at ease with reporters while downgrading his chances of winning. "Mark McGwire is in a different world," said Sosa. "He's the man, he's the guy everybody is looking for [to break the record]."[144] Sosa also said he did not feel pressured to break the record. "Pressure was for me," he would say, "when I was a shoeshine boy trying to make it to America."[145]

Milwaukee Brewers manager Phil Garner, whose team would play a big part in the record chase, said Sosa was smart to defer to McGwire. "I thought Sosa played it out well as the underdog," Garner said. "'Ah, he's The Man. I'm just along for the ride.' It took some of the pressure off him."[146]

The humor, goodwill, and grace with which both players conducted their historic quest was the best thing that happened to baseball in years. The players' strike in 1994, which cut short that season and postponed the start of the next, had alienated many fans. But with McGwire and Sosa popping home runs almost daily in a tight race for the record, baseball's popularity soared.

People who never cared for the game were enchanted that Sosa, after hitting a home run, would honor his mother by tapping his heart twice and blowing a kiss to the cameras, that he seemed happy McGwire was doing well, that he wasn't jealous when McGwire kept pulling ahead. Writes Sosa biographer Patricia J. Duncan:

The 1998 season was a display of what the power of the home run together with the power of the human spirit are capable of producing. Sammy Sosa's exceptional talent and his remarkable human qualities have united people of many different backgrounds. He brought a new flavor to America's pastime. Sammy Sosa has united the sport of baseball and brought together people of different classes, races and countries in a celebration of the human spirit.[147]

And in a nation often divided by racial animosity, both players were cheered by white and African American fans. In a *Time* magazine article headlined "Mi Amigo Mark" that carried his byline, Sosa wrote: "Some tried to suggest that our popularity was divided along racial lines. I never felt that at all. Everywhere I played, people of all races greeted me warmly and cheered me on, just as people of all races cheered for Mark."[148]

Down to the Wire—Home Runs and the Playoffs

When the two teams played in Chicago on August 19, Sosa took the lead for the first time with his 48th home run only to have McGwire tie him fifty-eight minutes later and go ahead in the tenth inning with his 49th. When they went into September tied at 55, excitingly close to the record with a month left to play, their quest became a national sensation.

On September 5 when McGwire became only the third player to hit 60 home runs, he said, "He [Sosa] motivates me. I motivate him. And this is fun. We're pushing each other. We're not going to stop now. We're doing a great job together."[149] McGwire beat Sosa to the historic figures of 61 and 62 in two dramatic games in St. Louis on September 7 and 8. But Sosa, stuck at 58 since September 5, would soon catch him, thanks to his "lucky team."

Sosa, pictured here rounding the bases after his sixtieth home run, said he and Mark McGwire motivated each other.

In 1998 the Brewers, the team Aaron finished his career with, surrendered a dozen home runs in forty-five at bats to Sosa (only four to McGwire), the most a player had hit against one club since 1961 when Maris belted thirteen against the White Sox. Sosa reached 60 on September 12 with a three-run homer off Milwaukee's Valerio de los Santos in a 13–11 win in Chicago and the next night homered off Bronswell Patrick and Eric Plunk to reach 62 in a wild 11–10 victory.

Although Sosa said the victories were more important than the home runs because they helped the Cubs stay alive in the playoff race, his 62nd tied McGwire and amazed him: "For the first time, I'm so emotional. I have to say it was something unbelievable, something I can't believe what I'm doing. I said to Mark McGwire [the night he got to 62], 'Wait for me.' Now we're together."[150] When McGwire went ahead again two days later with a homer in an 8–6 loss to Pittsburgh, he said he wouldn't be upset if Sosa won the race. "No," he said, "because what Sammy and I have done is fantastic."[151]

The Brewers helped Sosa tie McGwire again at 65 when Sosa hit two in one game in Milwaukee, and Sosa reached 66 first on September 25 only to have McGwire join him forty-five minutes later. It was the twenty-first time they had homered on the same day and the fourth time they had been tied since McGwire broke Maris's record.

After trailing McGwire early 24–9, Sosa outhomered him 57–46 from May 25 through the end of the season. But while Big Mac struck four more times in the final weekend, Sosa failed to homer again even though he had an extra 163rd game. On the Monday after the season ended, the Cubs played the San Francisco Giants because they were tied for the final playoff spot with identical 89–73 records.

In the game Sosa hit a pair of singles to help the Cubs win 5–3 and accomplish a team goal he valued over the home run title. "Tonight," he said, "I forgot about the home run. I just wanted to win."[152] Unfortunately for Sosa, his dream season ended with three straight losses as the Atlanta Braves swept Chicago in the first round of the playoffs. Sosa had only three hits in eleven at bats, none of them homers.

Sammy "Claus"—Most Valuable Person

Although Sosa lost to McGwire, his historic season did not go unhonored by baseball. On September 20 in a sold-out game at Wrigley Field, Baseball Commissioner Allan "Bud" Selig presented him with baseball's Historic Achievement Award. The ceremony was an emotional tribute to Sosa, who cried and said he loved Chicago before running a victory lap around the stadium to the cheers of fans, who had draped the park with Dominican Republic flags. Sosa also won the National League Most Valuable Player (MVP) award over McGwire because he had a higher average and more RBI while helping his team to postseason play.

To many observers, MVP also stood for Most Valuable Person because of Sosa's dedication to helping his native country and American children struggling in the same poverty he had grown up in. When Hurricane Georges struck his homeland in September, killing

First Lady Hillary Rodham Clinton admires a Cubs hat that Sosa autographed for her. Even the Dominican envoy to the United States credits Sosa with being his country's real ambassador.

hundreds and leaving thousands homeless, Sosa immediately began raising funds to help victims despite the historic home run race. He even helped load supplies bound for the Dominican Republic after a game in Houston, Texas. His foundation funneled trailers full of medicine, food, and clothing to his homeland, including forty tons of food in October alone. "I'm prouder of the rebuilding effort than I am of all my home runs,"[153] Sosa would say months later.

The hurricane relief, however, is just part of Sosa's charitable work. Sosa built the 30-30 Plaza in San Pedro de Macoris to give his hometown an economic boost—money thrown into a fountain in front of the plaza is given to shoeshine boys—and a charitable foundation he started in 1997 has already donated 250 computers to Dominican schools. Sosa is also known as "Sammy Claus" for his tours in the United States and Dominican Republic distributing thousands of gifts to children in schools and hospitals. Bernardo Vega, the Dominican ambassador to the United States, says Sosa is far more than just an athlete: "As far as I'm concerned, he's the real Dominican ambassador. I just shuffle papers."[154]

And that title is even more important to Sosa than that of Home Run King.

Home Run "Déjà Vu"

As Hall of Fame catcher Yogi Berra once said, "It's like déjà vu all over again."[155] The former New York Yankee great, famed for the bizarre spin he inflicts on familiar phrases, voiced those words decades ago. But in 1999 his tortured phraseology was a perfect fit for what one newspaper nicknamed "Home Run Derby II."

Because even Babe Ruth never hit 60 home runs two years in a row, the baseball world was simply not prepared when Mark McGwire and Sammy Sosa renewed their assault on the home run record book by becoming the first to top the magic mark in consecutive seasons. McGwire would finish first again with 65 home runs, just two more than Sosa.

"I think power hitting is a God-given talent," McGwire said in trying to explain their ability to keep hitting home runs at a record pace, "and I think the Man Upstairs has given us the talent to do that. We're all here for a purpose, and the purpose for Sammy and I is to do what we're doing right now."[156]

And that was to hit more home runs for the second straight year than anyone believed possible.

McGwire, Sosa Start Slow

During the off-season McGwire kept far away from the media that had dogged him for months. He spent time with his son, Matthew, relaxed at his home south of Los Angeles, California, and visited Australia with Ali Dickson, the six-foot former college volleyball player he has dated for several years.

But Sosa, reveling in his new fame, was more visible and even accepted an invitation from President Bill Clinton to attend his January State of the Union address. As television cameras recorded his reaction while he sat next to First Lady Hillary Clinton, Sosa heard the president say: "Sports records are made, and sooner or later, they're broken. But making other peoples' lives better, and showing our children the true meaning of brotherhood—that lasts forever. So for more than baseball, Sammy Sosa, you're a hero in two countries tonight."[157]

Although McGwire hit a home run in the April 5 opener, a 10–8 loss to the Milwaukee Brewers, he and Sosa got off to a slow start in 1999. McGwire had only five home runs at the end of April and Sosa four to trail Jose Canseco, McGwire's "Bash Brother" from Oakland. Now playing for the Tampa Bay Devil Rays, Canseco led the major leagues with ten heading into May. Asked about breaking the home run record, Canseco responded, "I'm not a robot. Only a robot like McGwire can do that [hit 70]."[158]

Canseco's words were prophetic. He was still leading in early July with 31 home runs when his all-too-human body broke down and back surgery sidelined him for more than a month. But as the season progressed, McGwire and Sosa, seemingly invulnerable to injury and opposing pitchers, once again left their competitors far behind.

Only this time, Sosa was "the man" as he led McGwire most of the season.

The Race Warms Up

On August 5 McGwire reached a historic milestone, hitting two home runs against San Diego to total 44 for the season and 501

Sosa stands next to Hillary Rodham Clinton at the 1999 State of the Union address. During his address, President Clinton saluted the Dominican slugger.

for his career. Only the sixteenth player to top 500, McGwire reached that mark faster than anyone—in just 5,487 at bats, 314 fewer than Ruth and an incredible 1,500 less than any other player. "I'm very proud of that," McGwire said. "I've exceeded everything I expected of myself."[159]

The two home runs pushed McGwire into the lead by three home runs, but Sosa picked up the pace and led McGwire by four—55 to 51—heading into September. Sosa had the same number of home runs as he had on August 31 in 1998 while McGwire was four behind his record pace of a year earlier. Even though McGwire's record appeared in jeopardy, the news media seemed bored with their home runs, which was fine with Sosa. "One of the reasons why there was a lot of media last year was because we were trying to break a record that was there for 37 years," he explained. "I like it the way it is now. It's quiet. It's cool."[160]

Mark McGwire examines a trophy that commemorates his 500 home runs.

The fans who had gone crazy over their exploits a year earlier also seemed to have lost interest. Maybe it's because they knew the balls they were hitting for home runs would not be worth a lot of money, as they had been when the two broke the record in 1998. The ball McGwire hit for his 70th home run, which was caught in the outfield seats by Philip Ozersky, was sold at an auction on January 12, 1999, for $2.7 million. The previous record price for a home run ball had been $126,500 for the one Ruth hit the day Yankee Stadium opened.

The 1999 Home Run King

On September 18 Sosa hit his 60th to become the first to reach that figure for two straight years. Naturally it came against his "lucky team," the Brewers. "A lot of people said at the beginning of the year it would be impossible to hit 60 two years in a row. Here I am,"[161] said Sosa, who admitted he was happy to reach it before McGwire, who a year earlier had beaten him to all the milestones.

Sosa also hit his 61st against Milwaukee the next day, but McGwire countered with two to trim Sosa's lead to three. When Sosa only hit two more in his last eleven games, McGwire came on strong to beat him for the second straight year. The race came down to a season-ending, three-game series in St. Louis. Fittingly both players homered in the finale, a 9–5 St. Louis victory in a contest halted in the fifth inning due to rain.

Are Home Runs Cheaper Today?

McGwire said he and Sosa hit so many home runs because they worked harder than other players. "The work ethic has to be dead-on every day," he said. "Only Sammy and I know what it feels like."[162] But some baseball analysts believe the game has entered a new era, one in which home runs are easier to hit. In 1999 homers flew out of ballparks at a phenomenal pace—5,528 in 2,428 games for an average of 2.28 home runs per game to shatter the record of 2.19 set in 1996. The reasons cited include weaker pitching due to expansion, a livelier ball, smaller ballparks, and a general increase in the size, strength, and overall conditioning of players.

Despite those factors, McGwire and Sosa once again greatly outdistanced their competition. Ken Griffey Jr. of Seattle led the American League with just 48 home runs and Chipper Jones of Atlanta finished third in the National League with 45, eighteen behind Sosa and twenty in back of McGwire.

The general consensus is that even if home runs are easier to hit, McGwire and Sosa are still in a class by themselves, so powerful that they could put up record numbers in any season. "You can't say it's because everybody's hitting home runs," explains Cubs' first baseman Mark Grace, who has watched Sosa slug his way through two historic seasons. "They're so far ahead of everybody else. My hat's off to them."[163]

Their home run prowess, however, did not help their teams very much in 1999. The Cardinals finished 75–86 and the Cubs, just a year after making the playoffs, nearly became the first team in history with fewer victories than their star hitter had home runs as they plummeted to a dismal mark of 67–95.

The Greatest?

Ruth, Maris, McGwire, and Sosa are the only players with 60 home runs in one season and Hank Aaron hit more (755) than anyone else. They are all Home Run Kings, but which one is the greatest of all?

Even modern ballplayers acknowledge that the legend of Babe Ruth overshadows them.

After watching McGwire and Sosa, today's fans find it hard to believe anyone was ever more powerful, but Hall of Fame pitcher Bob Feller disagrees. "If the Babe was playing today," said Feller, "he'd hit 75 homers. The ball is livelier, the pitching is spread thin [because there are more teams], and the strike zone is smaller."[164] Feller also notes that Aaron needed over three thousand more at bats than Ruth to top 714 home runs.

However, it is an exercise in futility to compare players from different eras because there are so many factors to consider—the quality of pitching, size of parks they play in, liveliness of the ball, changing nature of the game, and the comparative size and strength of the players. The debate will continue as long as baseball is played, but the mantle of the Greatest Home Run Hitter will probably always be decided not on fact but personal opinion.

And the unique mystique that has always enveloped the Babe will likely continue to help him overwhelm "pretenders" to his throne. After breaking Ruth's career home run record, Aaron admitted, "The legend of Babe Ruth is indestructible. It won't matter whether I hit 800 homers. There will never be another Babe Ruth as far as the baseball public is concerned."[165]

Sosa also knows Ruth's continuing hold on fans. "Babe Ruth is still alive," Sosa joked during the 1998 season. "He never died. Everybody remembers Babe Ruth like it was yesterday."[166] Even McGwire has wistfully said, "I wish I could go back and play with him [Ruth]."[167]

So long live the Babe—the past, present, and future Sultan of Swat!

NOTES

Introduction: From the "Babe" to "Big Mac"

1. Quoted in Robert W. Creamer, *Babe: The Legend Comes to Life.* New York: Simon & Schuster, 1974, p. 152.
2. Donald Honig, *Baseball America: The Heroes of the Game and the Times of Their Glory.* New York: Macmillan, 1985, p. 137.
3. William F. McNeil, *The King of Swat: An Analysis of Baseball's Home Run Hitters from the Major, Minor, Negro and Japanese Leagues.* Jefferson, NC: McFarland & Company, 1997, p. 1.
4. Tim McCarver with Danny Peary, *The Perfect Season: Why 1998 Was Baseball's Greatest Year.* New York: Villard Books, 1999, p. 13.

Chapter 1: Baseball: The National Pastime

5. Honig, *Baseball America*, p. 9.
6. Baseball Hall of Fame Web site, www.baseballhalloffame.org/members/hofers/ajc/ajc.html.
7. Quoted in Honig, *Baseball America*, p. 1.
8. Quoted in George B. Kirsch, "Bats, Balls, and Bullets," *Civil War Times Illustrated*, May 1998, p. 34.
9. Quoted in Kirsch, "Bats, Balls, and Bullets," p. 36.
10. John Stewart Bowman and Joel Zoss, *The American League: A History.* New York: Gallery Books, 1986, p. 8.
11. Mark Ribowsky, *A Complete History of the Negro Leagues, 1884 to 1955.* New York: Carol Publishing, 1995, p. 33.
12. Quoted in John Stewart Bowman and Joel Zoss, *The National League: A History.* New York: Gallery Books, 1986, p. 19.
13. Quoted in Ribowsky, *A Complete History of the Negro Leagues,* p. 32.
14. McNeil, *The King of Swat*, p. 132.
15. Quoted in Honig, *Baseball America*, p. 251.
16. McNeil, *The King of Swat*, p. 30.
17. Quoted in Creamer, *Babe*, p. 61.
18. Quoted in Bowman and Zoss, *The American League*, p. 32.
19. Quoted in George Sullivan, *Sluggers: Twenty-seven of Baseball's Greatest.* New York: Atheneum, 1991, p. 2.

Chapter 2: Babe Ruth: The Greatest Player Ever

20. Quoted in Alan Minsky, *Home Run Kings.* New York: MetroBooks, 1996, p. 22.

21. Quoted in Bowman and Zoss, *The American League,* p. 36.

22. Honig, *Baseball America,* p. 120.

23. Quoted in Sullivan, *Sluggers,* p. 61.

24. Quoted in Fred Lieb, *Baseball as I Have Known It.* New York: Coward, McCann & Geohegan, 1977, p. 154.

25. Quoted in Bob Allen with Bill Gilbert, *The 500 Home Run Club: Baseball's 15 Greatest Home Run Hitters from Aaron to Williams.* Champaign, IL: Sports Publishing, 1999, p. 216.

26. Quoted in Creamer, *Babe,* p. 37.

27. Quoted in Lois P. Nicholson, *Babe Ruth: Sultan of Swat.* Woodbury, CT: Goodwood Press, 1994, p. 24.

28. Quoted in Creamer, *Babe,* p. 196.

29. Quoted in Nicholson, *Babe Ruth,* p. 49.

30. Quoted in Allen with Gilbert, *The 500 Home Run Club,* p. 214.

31. Quoted in William Nack, "The Colossus," *Sports Illustrated,* August 8, 1998, p. 69.

32. Quoted in Nicholson, *Babe Ruth,* p. 96.

33. Quoted in Creamer, *Babe,* p. 255.

34. Quoted in Honig, *Baseball America,* p. 138.

35. Quoted in Honig, *Baseball America,* p. 139.

36. Quoted in Allen with Gilbert, *The 500 Home Run Club,* p. 220.

37. Quoted in Creamer, *Babe,* p. 222.

38. Quoted in Charles Einstein, ed., *The Baseball Reader: Favorites from the Fireside Books of Baseball.* New York: Lippincott & Crowell, 1980, p. 43.

39. Quoted in Nicholson, *Babe Ruth,* p. 87.

40. Quoted in Minsky, *Home Run Kings,* p. 59.

41. Quoted in Minsky, *Home Run Kings,* p. 59.

42. Quoted in Allen with Gilbert, *The 500 Home Run Club,* p. 225.

43. Quoted in Nicholson, *Babe Ruth,* p. 100.

44. Lieb, *Baseball as I Have Known It,* p. 153.

45. Quoted in Nicholson, *Babe Ruth,* p. 104.

46. Quoted in Minsky, *Home Run Kings,* p. 22.

Chapter 3: Roger Maris: Battling the Legend of the Babe

47. Quoted in McCarver with Peary, *The Perfect Season,* p. 134.

48. Quoted in Allen with Gilbert, *The 500 Home Run Club,* p. 229.

49. Quoted in Harvey Rosenfeld, *Roger Maris: A Title to Fame.* Fargo, ND: Prairie House, 1991, p. 19.

50. Quoted in Maury Allen, *Roger Maris: A Man for All Seasons.* New York: Donald J. Fine, 1986, p. 36.

51. Quoted in Rosenfeld, *Roger Maris,* p. 29.

52. Quoted in Rosenfeld, *Roger Maris,* p. 24.

53. Quoted in Allen, *Roger Maris,* p. 89.

54. Quoted in Allen, *Roger Maris,* p. 105.

55. Quoted in Rosenfeld, *Roger Maris,* p. 49.

56. Quoted in Allen, *Roger Maris,* p. 51.

57. Roger Maris and Jim Ogle, *Roger Maris at Bat.* New York: Duell, Sloan and Pearce, 1962, p. 8.

58. Quoted in Minsky, *Home Run Kings,* p. 45.

59. Maris and Ogle, *Roger Maris at Bat,* p. 55.

60. McCarver with Peary, *The Perfect Season,* p. 137.

61. Maris and Ogle, *Roger Maris at Bat,* p. 8.

62. Quoted in Alan Schwarz, "The Man Behind the Myth," *Sport,* October 1998, p. 82.

63. Mickey Mantle with Herb Gluck, *The Mick.* New York: Doubleday, 1985, p. 193.

64. Quoted in Susan M. McKinney, ed., *Home Run! The Year the Records Fell.* Champaign, IL: Sports Publishing, 1998, p. 73.

65. Quoted in Allen, *Roger Maris,* p. 137.

66. Quoted in Rosenfeld, *Roger Maris,* p. 83.

67. Maris and Ogle, *Roger Maris at Bat,* p. 156.

68. Quoted in Allen, *Roger Maris,* p. 100.

69. Quoted in Rosenfeld, *Roger Maris,* p. 127.

70. Quoted in Maris and Ogle, *Roger Maris at Bat,* p. 217.

71. Mantle with Gluck, *The Mick,* p. 196.

72. Quoted in Schwarz, "The Man Behind the Myth," p. 82.

73. Quoted in Allen, *Roger Maris,* p. 228.

Chapter 4: Hank Aaron: Breaking a Record and Defeating Bigotry

74. Quoted in Bill Koenig, "Aaron's Legacy Simply Homeric," *USA Today Baseball Weekly,* February 3–9, 1999, p. 8.

75. Quoted in Hank Aaron with Lonnie Wheeler, *I Had a Hammer: The Hank Aaron Story.* New York: HarperCollins, 1991, p. 231.

76. Quoted in Murray Chass, "At Long Last, Aaron Basks and the Fans Love It," *New York Times,* April 8, 1999, p. D1.

77. Aaron with Wheeler, *I Had a Hammer,* p. 8.

78. Aaron with Wheeler, *I Had a Hammer,* p. 15.

79. Henry Aaron with Furman Bisher, *Aaron.* New York: Thomas Crowell, 1974, p. 3.

80. Quoted in Allen with Gilbert, *The 500 Home Run Club,* p. 2.

81. Quoted in Tim Wendel, "Aaron: Blacks Priced Out of Ballpark," *USA Today Baseball Weekly*, February 3–9, 1999, p. 11.

82. Aaron with Wheeler, *I Had a Hammer,* p. 41.

83. Quoted in Aaron with Bisher, *Aaron,* p. 23.

84. Aaron with Bisher, *Aaron,* p. 35.

85. Henry Aaron, interview with author, July 20, 1999.

86. Aaron with Wheeler, *I Had a Hammer,* p. 133.

87. Aaron with Wheeler, *I Had a Hammer,* p. 134.

88. Aaron with Bisher, *Aaron,* p. 133.

89. Quoted in George Sullivan, *Sluggers,* p. 22.

90. Quoted in Allen with Gilbert, *The 500 Home Run Club,* p. 2.

91. Aaron with Bisher, *Aaron,* p. 206.

92. Quoted in George Plimpton, "Final Turn of the Drama," *Sports Illustrated,* April 4, 1994 (reprint of an article from April 1974), p. 99.

93. Aaron, interview with author, July 20, 1999.

94. Aaron, interview with author, July 20, 1999.

95. Quoted in Aaron, interview with author, July 20, 1999.

96. Bob Allen, interview with author, August 31, 1999.

97. Quoted in Koenig, "Aaron's Legacy Simply Homeric," p. 10.

98. Quoted in Allen with Gilbert, *The 500 Home Run Club,* p. 14.

99. Quoted in Steve Meyerhoff, Bob Rose, Mike Smith, editorial directors, *Celebrating 70: Mark McGwire's Historic Season*. St. Louis: Sporting News Publishing, 1998, p. 46.

100. Quoted in Alex Tresniowski et al., "A Truly Grand Slam," *People,* September 21, 1998, p. 180.

101. Quoted in Daniel Okrent, "A Mac for All Seasons," *Time,* December 28, 1998, p. 140.

102. Quoted in Tom Verducci, "Making His Mark," *Sports Illustrated,* September 14, 1998, p. 32.

103. Quoted in McKinney, *Home Run!,* p. 86.

104. Quoted in Rob Rains, *Mark McGwire: Home Run Hero.* New York: St. Martin's Press, 1998, p. 13.

105. Quoted in Tom Verducci, "Sportsmen of the Year, Stroke of Genius," *Sports Illustrated,* December 21, 1998, p. 48.

106. McCarver with Peary, *The Perfect Season,* p. 5.

107. Quoted in Rains, *Mark McGwire,* p. 106.

108. Quoted in Rick Reilly, "The Good Father," *Sports Illustrated,* September 7, 1998, p. 38.

109. Quoted in Reilly, "The Good Father," p. 38.

110. Quoted in Reilly, "The Good Father," p. 40.

111. Quoted in Ken Daley, "Mark McGwire: Baseball's Most Prolific Home Run Hitter," *Baseball Digest,* December 1998, p. 62.

112. Quoted in McKinney, *Home Run!,* p. 17.

113. Quoted in McKinney, *Home Run!,* p. 21.

114. Quoted in Meyerhoff, Rose, Smith, *Celebrating 70,* p. 24.

115. Quoted in Tom Verducci, "Man on a Mission," *Sports Illustrated,* April 7, 1998, p. 78.

116. Quoted in McKinney, *Home Run!,* p. 66.

117. Quoted in Gary Smith, "Home Run Fever," *Sports Illustrated,* August 3, 1998, pp. 42–43.

118. Quoted in McKinney, *Home Run!,* p. 92.

119. Mark McGwire with Tom Verducci, "Where Do I Go from Here," *Sports Illustrated,* September 21, 1998, p. 54.

120. Quoted in Meyerhoff, Rose, Smith, *Celebrating 70,* p. 86.

121. Quoted in Meyerhoff, Rose, Smith, *Celebrating 70*, p. 136.

122. McGwire with Verducci, "Where Do I Go from Here," p. 55.

123. Quoted in Meyerhoff, Rose, Smith, *Celebrating 70*, p. 152.

124. Quoted in Tom Verducci, "The Greatest Season Ever," *Sports Illustrated,* October 5, 1998, p. 43.

125. Quoted in Tresniowski et al., "A Truly Grand Slam," p. 182.

Chapter 6: Sammy Sosa: Happy with 66!

126. Quoted in Skip Bayless, *Sammy's Season.* Chicago: Contemporary Books, 1998, p. 7.

127. Quoted in Carrie Muskat, *Latinos in Baseball: Sammy Sosa.* Childs, MD: Mitchell Lane Publishers, 1999, p. 18.

128. Quoted in George Castle, *Sammy Sosa: Clearing the Vines.* Champaign, IL: Sports Publishing, 1998, p. 5.

129. Quoted in Muskat, *Sammy Sosa*, p. 19.

130. Quoted in Patricia J. Duncan, *Sosa! Baseball's Home Run Hero.* New York: Simon & Schuster, 1998, p. 32.

131. Quoted in Duncan, *Sosa!*, p. 34.

132. Quoted in Duncan, *Sosa!*, p. 37.

133. Quoted in Tom Verducci, "The Education of Sammy Sosa," *Sports Illustrated,* June 29, 1998, p. 43.

134. Quoted in Joel Stein, "Grand Sam," *Time,* September 28, 1998, p. 76.

135. Quoted in Richard Jerome et al., "'Sam I Am,'" *People,* September 9, 1998, p. 116.

136. Quoted in Castle, *Sammy Sosa*, p. 60.

137. Quoted in Muskat, *Sammy Sosa*, p. 36.

138. Quoted in Bayless, *Sammy's Season*, p. 6.

139. Quoted in Bayless, *Sammy's Season*, p. 6.

140. Quoted in Duncan, *Sosa!*, pp. 47–48.

141. Quoted in Verducci, "The Education of Sammy Sosa," p. 44.

142. Quoted in Castle, *Sammy Sosa*, p. 127.

143. Quoted in McKinney, *Home Run!*, p. 60.

144. Quoted in McKinney, *Home Run!*, p. 62.

145. Quoted in Jerome et al., "'Sam I Am,'" p. 116.

146. Phil Garner, interview with author, June 13, 1999.

147. Duncan, *Sosa!*, p. 14.

148. Sammy Sosa, "Mi Amigo Mark," *Time,* December 28, 1998, p. 142.

149. Quoted in Meyerhoff, Rose, Smith, *Celebrating 70,* p. 132.

150. Quoted in Meyerhoff, Rose, Smith, *Celebrating 70,* p. 157.

151. Quoted in Meyerhoff, Rose, Smith, *Celebrating 70,* p. 158.

152. Quoted in McKinney, *Home Run!,* p. 140.

153. Quoted in *Time International,* "Sammy Sosa, 30: A World-Class Sports Hero Who Has Brought Economic Muscle to Bear on His Homeland," May 24, 1999, p. 73.

154. Quoted in Castle, *Sammy Sosa,* p. 2.

Epilogue: Home Run "Déjà Vu"

155. Quoted in Deron Snyder, "Sammy and Mac: The Sequel," *USA Today Baseball Weekly,* August 11–17, 1999, p. 8.

156. Dave Van Dyck, "Sosa-McGwire: A Story Meant to Be Enjoyed," *Chicago Sun-Times,* September 21, 1999, p. 102.

157. Quoted in *Jet,* "Clinton Salutes Rosa Parks, Sammy Sosa During State of the Union Address," February 8, 1999, p. 14.

158. Quoted in Chip Scoggins, "Mark Canseco's Words, He's No McGwire," *Chicago Tribune,* April 28, 1999, sec. 4, p. 3.

159. Quoted in Michael Rosenberg, "Mac Passes Soar Spot," *Washington Post* story printed in the *Milwaukee Journal-Sentinel,* August 6, 1999, p. 1C.

160. Quoted in Tom Haudricourt, "Second Time Is the Charm," *Milwaukee Journal-Sentinel,* September 7, 1999, p. 4C.

161. Quoted in Paul Sullivan, "Sosa Connects; It's History," *Chicago Tribune,* September 19, 1999, sec. 4, pp. 1, 16.

162. Quoted in Mel Antonen, "McGwire, Sosa Each Take Final Shots," *USA Today,* October 4, 1999, p. 6C.

163. Quoted in Tom Verducci, "Blow for Blow," *Sports Illustrated,* August 23, 1999, p. 40.

164. Quoted in Bob Dolgan, "Babe Ruth: He Set the Standard for Today's Sluggers," *Baseball Digest,* December 1998, p. 52.

165. Quoted in Minsky, *Home Run Kings,* p. 18.

166. Quoted in Muskat, *Sammy Sosa,* p. 45.

167. Quoted in McKinney, *Home Run!,* p. 97.

CHRONOLOGY

June 19, 1846
The first game of baseball is played at Hoboken, New Jersey; the New York Nine defeats the Knickerbocker Baseball Club.

1859
Amherst College defeats Williams College in the first college game.

December 25, 1862
Two Union army All-Star teams play baseball before an estimated 40,000 soldiers, a crowd that may have been the largest to witness an athletic event in the nineteenth century.

1869
The Cincinnati Red Stockings, the first professional team, wins seventy-nine of eighty games and ties another in a series of contests from Long Island, New York, to San Francisco, California.

April 22, 1876
In the first National League (NL) game, Boston defeats Philadelphia 6–5.

1881
The pitcher's mound is moved back five feet so it is fifty feet away from home plate.

1884
A rule change allows pitchers, for the first time, to throw the ball overhand in professional baseball; up until then they had to throw underhand; Ned Williamson of the NL Chicago White Stockings hits a major league record of 27 home runs.

July 14, 1887
Owners in the International League, a minor league, meet in Buffalo, New York, and vote 6–4 to bar African Americans from the game; the ban was in effect until 1947.

1893
The pitcher's mound is moved back to its current distance of sixty feet six inches; the flat bat is banned.

April 24, 1901
In the first American League (AL) game, the Chicago White Sox defeat the Cleveland Bronchos (a team known today as the Indians) 8–2.

1903
The American League and National League merge, with each having eight teams; in the first World Series the AL Boston Pilgrims defeat the NL Pittsburgh Pirates by winning five out of eight games.

1910
A baseball with a cork center is introduced, leading to an increase in hitting and offense.

1914
The rival Federal League is organized to compete with the AL and NL major leagues. Despite luring some top players away from the two established leagues, it goes out of business after only two seasons of play.

1919
George Herman "Babe" Ruth Jr. sets a major league record with 29 home runs while playing for the Boston Red Sox.

1920
Rule changes that ban the spitball and other pitches tampering with the ball and introduction of a new "livelier" ball lead to a home run and offensive explosion; Ruth, now with the New York Yankees, nearly doubles his record to 54 home runs.

1921
Ruth increases his record to 59 home runs.

September 30, 1927
George Herman "Babe" Ruth Jr. hits his 60th home run to set a record that will last thirty-four years.

July 6, 1933
In the first All-Star Game at Comiskey Park in Chicago, Ruth hits the first home run in All-Star history to lead AL players to a 4–3 victory over the NL.

May 25, 1935
In one of his last games, Ruth hits three home runs for the Boston Braves.

April 15, 1947
Jackie Robinson plays for the Brooklyn Dodgers, becoming the first African American major leaguer in more than a half century.

April 19, 1958
The Los Angeles Dodgers and San Francisco Giants, which both moved to California from New York, play the first major league game on the West Coast.

October 1, 1961
Roger Maris of the New York Yankees hits his 61st home run to break Ruth's single-season record.

April 8, 1974
Hank Aaron of the Atlanta Braves hits his 715th home run to break Ruth's career home run record; Aaron hits his 755th and last homer on July 20, 1976, for the Milwaukee Brewers.

1998

Sammy Sosa of the Chicago Cubs hits a major league record 20 home runs in June; Mark McGwire of the St. Louis Cardinals hits his 61st home run on September 7 to tie Roger Maris; McGwire hits his 62nd home run on September 8 to break the record; Sosa becomes the first player to hit 66 home runs on September 25, but forty-five minutes later McGwire ties him; McGwire hits a pair of home runs in both of the last two games of the season, September 26 and 27, to finish with a record 70 home runs.

August 5, 1999

McGwire smashes two home runs to total 501 for his career, becoming only the sixteenth player to top 500 home runs; he reaches that historic mark more quickly than anyone ever had in just 5,487 at bats, 314 fewer than Ruth.

FOR FURTHER READING

Donald Honig, *Baseball America: The Heroes of the Game and the Times of Their Glory*. New York: Macmillan, 1985. An entertaining history of baseball that focuses on the players who made the game great.

Susan M. McKinney, ed., *Home Run! The Year the Records Fell*. Champaign, IL: Sports Publishing, 1998. Vividly dramatizes the 1998 home run race through stories and pictures compiled from files of the Associated Press.

Carrie Muskat, *Latinos in Baseball: Sammy Sosa*. Childs, MD: Mitchell Lane Publishers, 1999. A well-written biography of Sosa.

Lois P. Nicholson, *Babe Ruth: Sultan of Swat*. Woodbury, CT: Goodwood Press, 1994. A well-written biography for the younger reader.

Richard Scott Rennert, *Henry Aaron*. New York: Chelsea House Publishers, 1993. A solid biography of Aaron for younger readers.

Mark Ribowsky, *A Complete History of the Negro Leagues, 1884 to 1955*. New York: Carol Publishing Group, 1995. A detailed history of the Negro Leagues and their greatest players, including home run hitter Josh Gibson.

George Sullivan, *Sluggers: Twenty-seven of Baseball's Greatest*. New York: Atheneum, 1991. Brief biographies of the game's greatest hitters.

WORKS CONSULTED

Hank Aaron with Lonnie Wheeler, *I Had a Hammer: The Hank Aaron Story*. New York: HarperCollins, 1991. This autobiography provides a complete picture of Aaron's life, including his years after he broke Ruth's home run record.

Henry Aaron with Furman Bisher, *Aaron*. New York: Thomas Crowell, 1974. An autobiography that recounts Aaron's life through his record-breaking 1972 season.

Bob Allen with Bill Gilbert, *The 500 Home Run Club: Baseball's 15 Greatest Home Run Hitters from Aaron to Williams*. Champaign, IL: Sports Publishing, 1999. Individual biographies of the select group of players who have hit more than 500 home runs.

Maury Allen, *Roger Maris: A Man for All Seasons*. New York: Donald J. Fine, 1986. This New York sportswriter vividly captures the drama of Maris's chase of Ruth's record and how it affected his life.

Skip Bayless, *Sammy's Season*. Chicago: Contemporary Books, 1998. This book uses pictures and accompanying text for a daily recap of Sosa's 66 home runs.

John Stewart Bowman and Joel Zoss, *The American League: A History*. New York: Gallery Books, 1986. A comprehensive, easy-to-read history of the American League.

———, *The National League: A History*. New York: Gallery Books, 1986. A comprehensive, easy-to-read history of the National League.

George Castle, *Sammy Sosa: Clearing the Vines*. Champaign, IL: Sports Publishing, 1998. A book on the 1998 season that focuses as much on how the Cubs fared as did Sosa; non-Cub fans may find parts of it boring.

Robert W. Creamer, *Babe: The Legend Comes to Life*. New York: Simon & Schuster, 1974. This biography, the one that all others on Ruth are measured by, explains his life and personality better than any ever written.

Patricia J. Duncan, *Sosa! Baseball's Home Run Hero*. New York: Simon & Schuster, 1998. A solid biography of Sosa and his incredible 1998 season.

Charles Einstein, ed., *The Baseball Reader: Favorites from the Fireside Books of Baseball*. New York: Lippincott & Crowell, 1980. Collected articles and essays on baseball by famous writers.

Fred Lieb, *Baseball as I Have Known It*. New York: Coward, Mc-Cann & Geohegan, 1977. A baseball writer for more than a half century and a friend of Ruth's, Lieb provides interesting insights into Ruth and baseball.

Mickey Mantle with Herb Gluck, *The Mick*. New York: Doubleday, 1985. A solid autobiography by one of the game's greatest players.

Roger Maris and Jim Ogle, *Roger Maris at Bat*. New York: Duell, Sloan and Pearce, 1962. This book recounts, often in boring detail, each of Maris's 61 home runs, but fails to adequately address the controversy of his record season or inform the reader about his personality.

Tim McCarver with Danny Peary, *The Perfect Season: Why 1998 Was Baseball's Greatest Year*. New York: Villard Books, 1999. This former player, now a television analyst, provides interesting insights into what may have been baseball's greatest season.

Jeanne McClow, *A Baseball Century: The First 100 Years of the National League*. New York: Macmillan, 1976. Interesting facts make this a very readable book.

William F. McNeil, *The King of Swat: An Analysis of Baseball's Home Run Hitters from the Major, Minor, Negro and Japanese Leagues*. Jefferson, NC: McFarland & Company, 1997. An intriguing book that uses a variety of statisical analyses to compare the greatest home run hitters; recommended for people who like to crunch numbers.

Steve Meyerhoff, Bob Rose, Mike Smith, editorial directors, *Celebrating 70: Mark McGwire's Historic Season*. St. Louis: Sporting News Publishing, 1998. A solid account of McGwire's season taken from stories in the *Sporting News*.

Alan Minsky, *Home Run Kings*. New York: MetroBooks, 1996. Readable biographies of some of the top home run hitters of all time.

Rob Rains, *Mark McGwire: Home Run Hero*. New York: St. Martin's Press, 1998. A solid biography but one that was written before his record-setting 1998 season.

Harvey Rosenfeld, *Roger Maris: A Title to Fame*. Fargo, ND: Prairie House, 1991. An in-depth biography of Maris that is filled with great quotes from players and other people who knew Maris.

George Vecsey, *McGwire and Sosa: Baseball's Greatest Home Run Story*. New York: Welcome Rain, 1998. A short but concise look at the 1998 home run chase that is lavishly illustrated with color pictures.

Periodicals

Ken Daley, "Mark McGwire: Baseball's Most Prolific Home Run Hitter," *Baseball Digest*, December 1998, pp. 60–63.

Bob Dolgan, "Babe Ruth: He Set the Standard for Today's Sluggers," *Baseball Digest*, December 1998, pp. 48–52.

Richard Jerome et al., "'Sam I Am,'" *People*, September 9, 1998, pp. 115–16.

Jet, "Clinton Salutes Rosa Parks, Sammy Sosa During State of the Union Address," February 8, 1999, p. 14.

George B. Kirsch, "Bats, Balls, and Bullets," *Civil War Times Illustrated*, May 1998, pp. 30–37.

Mark McGwire with Tom Verducci, "Where Do I Go from Here," *Sports Illustrated*, September 21, 1998, pp. 52–55.

William Nack, "The Colossus," *Sports Illustrated*, August 8, 1998, pp. 58–70.

Daniel Okrent, "A Mac for All Seasons," *Time*, December 28, 1998, pp. 138–42.

George Plimpton, "Final Turn of the Drama," *Sports Illustrated*, April 4, 1994 (reprint of an article from April 1974), pp. 86–102.

Rick Reilly, "The Good Father," *Sports Illustrated*, September 7, 1998, pp. 32–45.

Alan Schwarz, "The Man Behind the Myth," *Sport*, October 1998, p. 82.

Gary Smith, "Home Run Fever," *Sports Illustrated*, August 3, 1998, pp. 42–50.

Sammy Sosa, "Mi Amigo Mark," *Time*, December 28, 1998, p. 142.

Joel Stein, "Grand Sam," *Time*, September 28, 1998, pp. 76–77.

Time International, "Sammy Sosa, 30: A World-Class Sports Hero Who Has Brought Economic Muscle to Bear on His Homeland," May 24, 1999, p. 73.

Alex Tresniowski et al., "A Truly Grand Slam," *People*, September 21, 1998, pp. 180–82.

Tom Verducci, "Blow for Blow," *Sports Illustrated*, August 23, 1999, pp. 38–44.

———, "The Education of Sammy Sosa," *Sports Illustrated*, June 29, 1998, pp. 37–44.

———, "The Greatest Season Ever," *Sports Illustrated*, October 5, 1998, pp. 38–52.

————, "Making His Mark," *Sports Illustrated*, September 14, 1998, pp. 28–33.

————, "Man on a Mission," *Sports Illustrated*, April 7, 1998, pp. 76–84.

————, "Sportsmen of the Year, Stroke of Genius," *Sports Illustrated*, December 21, 1998, pp. 40–72.

Newspapers

Mel Antonen, "McGwire, Sosa Each Take Final Shots," *USA Today*, October 4, 1999, p. 6C.

Murray Chass, "At Long Last, Aaron Basks and the Fans Love It," *New York Times*, April 8, 1999, sec. D, pp. 1, 3.

Tom Haudricourt, "Brewers, Bere Help Sosa Make History Again," *Milwaukee Journal-Sentinel*, September 19, 1999, sec. C, pp. 1, 17.

————, "McGwire Blasts a Typical Homer," *Milwaukee Journal*, April l6, 1999, sec. C, pp. 1, 7.

————, "Second Time Is the Charm," *Milwaukee Journal-Sentinel*, September 7, 1999, p. 4C.

Bill Koenig, "Aaron's Legacy Simply Homeric," *USA Today Baseball Weekly*, February 3–9, 1999, pp. 8, 10.

Michael Rosenberg, "Mac Passes Soar Spot," *Washington Post* story printed in the *Milwaukee Journal-Sentinel*, August 6, 1999, sec. C, pp. 1, 4.

Chip Scoggins, "Mark Canseco's Words, He's No McGwire," *Chicago Tribune*, April 28, 1999, sec. 4, p. 3.

Deron Snyder, "Sammy and Mac: The Sequel," *USA Today Baseball Weekly*, August 11–17, 1999, pp. 8, 10.

Paul Sullivan, "Sosa Connects; It's History," *Chicago Tribune*, September 19, 1999, sec. 4, pp. 1, 16.

Dave Van Dyck, "Sosa-McGwire: A Story Meant to Be Enjoyed," *Chicago Sun-Times*, September 21, 1999, p. 102.

Tim Wendel, "Aaron: Blacks Priced Out of Ballpark," *USA Today Baseball Weekly*, February 3–9, 1999, p. 11.

INDEX

Aaron, Estella (mother), 49
Aaron, Gail (son), 56
Aaron, Hank, Jr. (son), 56
Aaron, Henry Louis "Hank," 10–11,
  62, 88, 99
  Atlanta and, 55–56
  awards of, 50, 52–54, 59
  background of, 49
  Chasing the Dream Foundation, 59
  Eau Claire Bears and, 51–52
  home runs and, 53–54, 56, 88–90
  Indianapolis Clowns and, 50–51
  Milwaukee Braves and, 53–55
  Milwaukee Brewers and, 58–59
  personality of, 59
  racism and, 49, 51–53, 55, 57
  record of, 56–57
  Robinson and, 49–50
  Ruth and, 48, 56–59
Aaron, Herbert (father), 49
Aaron, Herbert, Jr. (brother), 52
Aaron, Lary (son), 56
African Americans, 17–18, 55, 98–99
  Aaron and, 49, 51–53, 55, 57
  Sosa and, 81
Agent Orange. See McGwire, Mark
A. J. Reach Company, 20, 29
Alaska Summer League, 62
Allen, Bob, 59
Allen, Maury, 43
All-Star Games, 33, 41–44, 52, 78,
  99
Alou, Felipe, 75
American League, The (Bowman and
  Zoss), 16
American League (AL), 9, 16–17, 27,
  88, 98
  Aaron and, 58
  expanded schedule of, 41
  home run records and, 28, 31
American Legion Baseball, 38, 61
Amherst College, 15, 98
Anchorage Glacier Pilots, 62
Andujar, Joaquin, 74
Anson, Adrian "Cap," 17
Arizona Diamondbacks, 66

Atlanta Braves, 10, 82, 99

Babe Ruth. See Ruth, George Herman
  "Babe"
Baker, Frank "Home Run," 9
Baltimore American (Pippen), 20
Baltimore Orioles, 25–26
Baltimore Terrapins, 25
Bambino. See Ruth, George Herman
  "Babe"
Barrow, Ed, 8, 27
baseball
  All-Star Games and, 33, 41–44, 52,
    78, 99
  beginnings of, 12–14, 18–20
  British influence and, 12–13
  chronology of, 98–100
  greatest Home Run King and,
    88–90
  Hall of Fame and, 13–14, 17–18,
    34–35, 59
  Home Run Derby II and, 85–88
  lively ball and, 20–21, 29, 88–89,
    99
  new rules and, 29
  pitching and, 18–19, 98
  popularity of, 12, 14–15
  professional, 15–17
  racial issues and, 11, 17–18
  rowdiness of, 16
  see also home runs
Baseball America (Honig), 12
Bash Brothers, 64, 86
Beck, Rod, 79
Bell, George, 76
"Bellyache Heard Around the World,
  The," 31
Bennett, Shayne, 69
Berra, Yogi, 85
Big Mac. See McGwire, Mark
Billingham, Jack, 56
Bishop Shanley High School, 37
Black Sox scandal, 20, 29
Bodie, Ping, 31
Boston Braves, 33, 49, 99
Boston Pilgrims, 17, 98

Boston Red Sox, 8, 20, 99
  Ruth and, 26–28
bowler (pitcher), 13
Bowman, John Stewart, 16
Bronx stadium, 30
Brooklyn Atlantics, 16
Brooklyn Dodgers, 27, 49, 55, 99
  racial issues and, 17
Brother Matthias, 25
Broun, Heywood, 32
Burdette, Lew, 53–54
Burnside, Pete, 40–41

Cannon, Jimmy, 47
Canseco, Jose, 64, 86
Carrigan, Bill, 27
Cartwright, Alexander Joy, 13–14
Carvell, Pat, 38
Castilla, Vinnie, 67
Cerv, Bob, 43
Chase, Bill, 74–75
Chase, Debbie, 75
Chicago Cubs, 10, 17, 28, 32, 41, 88
  Cardinals and, 69–70
  Sosa and, 76–79, 82, 100
Chicago White Sox, 16, 98
  scandal of, 20, 29
  Sosa and, 76
Chicago White Stockings, 17, 28, 98
Cincinnati Red Stockings, 15–16, 98
Civil War, 14–15
Clemens, Roger, 76
Cleveland Bronchos, 16, 98
Cleveland Indians, 16, 38
  Maris and, 38–39
Clinton, Bill, 85–86
Clinton, Hillary, 83, 85–86
Cobb, Ty, 59
Colorado Rockies, 67
Comiskey, Charles, 16
Comiskey Park, 99
*Complete History of the Negro
  Leagues, A* (Ribowsky), 17
Connor, Roger, 29
Considine, Bob, 31
County Stadium (Milwaukee), 54
Craft, Harry, 39
Cravath, Gavvy, 28
cricket, 12

Davidson, Bob, 72

Dedeaux, Rod, 62
de los Santos, Valerio, 82
Detroit Tigers, 41, 58
Dickson, Ali, 85
DiMaggio, Joe, 41
Dominican Republic, 74–75
  Hurricane Georges and, 83–84
Doubleday, Abner, 14
Downing, Al, 57
Drago, Dick, 58
Duncan, Patricia J., 80–81
Dunn, Jack, 25

Eldred, Cal, 79
Esquela, Chico, 73
Esther, Sonia, 77–78

Fargo Central High School, 37
Fargo-Morehead team, 38
Federal League, 25, 99
Feller, Bob, 89
Fisher, Jack, 45
Florida Marlins, 67
Foxx, Jimmie, 41
Frazee, Harry, 28
Frick, Ford, 10, 41–42
Fulton County Stadium, 56

Garner, Horace, 52
Garner, Phil, 80
Gehrig, Lou, 31
Gibson, Josh, 17
Grace, Mark, 88
Greenberg, Hank, 41
Griffey, Ken, Jr., 67–69, 80, 88
Griggs, Dewey, 51
Grimm, Charlie, 53
Guerrero, Pedro, 74
Gulf Coast Rookie League, 75

Hammerin' Hank. *See* Aaron, Henry
  Louis "Hank"
Hartwell Field, 50
Hoboken, New Jersey, 13
Hodgson, Claire Merritt, 31–32, 34
Hodgson, Julia, 32
Home Run Derby II, 85–88
Home Run King. *See* Ruth, George
  Herman "Babe"
home runs
  Aaron and, 53–54, 56, 88–90

best year of, 10–11
greatest Home Run King and, 88–90
Home Run Derby II and, 85–88
Maris and, 36, 39–42, 44–46, 88–90
McGwire and, 62–63, 65–72, 85–90
modern ease of, 88
new rules and, 20, 29
1999 King and, 87–88
prejudice and, 10
Ruth and, 8–9, 20–23, 29, 32–33, 40–41, 88–90
Sosa and, 78–82, 85–90
as theater, 8–9
Honig, Donald, 8, 12, 24
Hooper, Harry, 8
Hoover, Herbert, 23
Hornsby, Rogers, 19
Houk, Ralph, 44
"House That Ruth Built, The," 30
Hughes, Kathy, 62, 64
Hulbert, William A., 16
Hurricane Georges, 74, 83–84
Huston, Tillinghast, 29
Hutton, Mark, 78

Indianapolis Clowns, 50
International League, 17, 26, 98
Isaacson, Julius, 39–40

Jackson, Reggie, 66
Jacksonville Journal, 53
Johnson, Byron Banford, 16
Jones, Chipper, 88
Jordan, Michael, 23

Kansas City Royals, 39
Kennedy, John F., 46
King of Swat, The (McNeil), 9, 19
Knickerbocker Baseball Club, 13–14, 98
Kuhn, Bowie, 56, 59

Lander's Coffee Shop, 26
Landis, Kennesaw Mountain, 31
Lardner, Ring, 21
Leonard, Buck, 18
Lieb, Fred, 34
Lincoln, Abraham, 14

Literary Digest, 22
Logan, Johnny, 53–54
Los Angeles Dodgers, 57, 99
Los Angeles Times, 63
Lucas, Barbara, 53

M&M Boys, 41
MacPhail, Andrew B., 79
Mantilla, Felix, 52, 55
Mantle, Mickey, 33, 39, 46–47, 56, 63
  home runs and, 41
  Maris and, 43–44
  Ruth and, 41–42
Maras, Connie Sturbitz (mother), 36
Maras, Roger Eugene. *See* Maris, Roger
Maras, Rudy, Jr. (brother), 37, 47
Maras, Rudy, Sr. (father), 36
March, Jerry, 37
Marco Solo. *See* McGwire, Mark
Marichal, Juan, 75
Maris, Kevin (son), 40
Maris, Pat (wife), 46
Maris, Randy (son), 40
Maris, Rich (son), 40
Maris, Roger, 9–11, 60–61, 82, 99–100
  awards of, 40
  background of, 36–38
  final years of, 47
  Frick ruling and, 41–42
  home runs and, 36, 39–42, 44–46, 88–90
  M&M Boys and, 41
  major leagues and, 38–39
  Mantle and, 43–44
  McGwire and, 63, 70–71
  media and, 43–44, 46–47, 68
  minor leagues and, 38
  personality of, 39–40, 43
  Ruth record and, 36, 40–42, 44
  strain on, 45–47
Maris, Roger, Jr. (son), 40, 71
Maris, Sandra (daughter), 40
Maris, Susan (daughter), 39–40
Mark McGwire Foundation, 66
Mathews, Eddie, 53, 56
Mays, Willie, 56
McCarver, Tim, 11, 43, 63
McGwire, Dan (brother), 61

McGwire, Ginger (mother), 61
McGwire, John (father), 61
McGwire, Mark, 10–11, 100
  awards of, 62–63
  background of, 61–62
  batting and, 61–65
  fast start of, 66–68
  home runs and, 62–63, 65–72,
    85–90
  media and, 63, 68
  minors and, 62–63
  moonshots and, 67
  Olympics and, 62
  pitching and, 61–62
  problems of, 64–67
  son and, 60–61, 64–65, 71, 85
  Sosa and, 69–71, 80–82
McGwire, Matthew (son), 60–61,
  64–65, 71, 85
  as batboy, 66–67
McNeil, William F., 9, 18–19
"Mi Amigo Mark" (Sosa), 81
Mills Commission, 14
Milwaukee Braves, 51
  Aaron and, 53–55
  1958 World Series and, 55
Milwaukee Brewers, 86–88, 99
  Aaron and, 58–59
  Sosa and, 79–82
Milwaukee County Stadium, 56
Milwaukee Journal, 55
Minaya, Omar, 76
Minnesota Twins, 76
Montero, Bautista, 74
Montero, Lucrecia, 74–75
Montreal Expos, 62
Morandini, Mickey, 79
Morgan, Mike, 70
Morris, Garrett, 73
Muffett, Billy, 54

National Association of Professional
  Baseball Players, 16
National League (NL), 16–17, 27, 98
  Aaron and, 50
  home runs and, 28, 70
  McGwire and, 66
  1951 pennant and, 53
  1957 pennant and, 53
Negro Leagues, 17–18, 50–51
Newark Daily Journal, 17

New York ball (game), 13
New York Clipper, 15
New York Giants, 17, 30
New York Nine, 13, 98
New York Post, 43
New York World, 32
New York Yankees, 8, 26, 54
  home runs and, 9
  Mantle and, 44
  Maris and, 39, 41, 46–47
  1958 World Series and, 55
  Ruth and, 29–33, 99
  Sosa and, 76
No, No, Nannette (play), 29

Oakland A's, 61–62
  World Series and, 64–65
Oh, Sadaharu, 58
Olympics, 62
one old cat (ball game), 12
Orange Crush. *See* McGwire, Mark
Ozersky, Philip, 87

Parque Duarte, 74
Patrick, Bronswell, 82
Patterson, Ken, 76
Pavano, Carl, 71
Pentland, Jeff, 79
Philadelphia Athletics, 9, 41
Pipp, Wally, 9
Pippen, Rodger, 20, 25
Pittsburgh Pirates, 17, 40, 98
Plunk, Eric, 82
Polo Grounds, 8, 30
Puerto Rican League, 53
Putnam, George H., 14

Reyes, Dennis, 70
Ribowsky, Mark, 17
Riggleman, Jim, 78
Robertson, Randy, 62
Robinson, Jackie, 17, 49, 99
Rodriguez, Henry, 79
Rose, Pete, 59
rounders (ball game), 12
Ruppert, Jacob, 29
Ruth, Dorothy (daughter), 31
Ruth, George Herman "Babe," 8,
  11, 61, 99
  background of, 23–25
  fans' loyalty to, 10, 41–42, 44

Gibson and, 17
greatest Home Run King and,
    88–90
hitting in Boston and, 27–28
"Home Run" Baker and, 9
home runs of, 8–9, 20–23, 29,
    32–33, 40–41
income of, 27, 30–31
last years of, 33–35
legend of, 29–33
Maris and, 36, 40–42, 44
McGwire and, 63
nicknames of, 25, 29
outfield and, 28
personality of, 23–24, 31–32
pitching and, 26–28, 33
Yankees and, 29–33, 99
Ruth, George Herman, Sr. (father), 24
Ruth, Margaret "Mamie" (sister), 24

St. Louis Cardinals, 10, 19, 88
    Cubs and, 69–70
    Maris and, 47
    McGwire and, 66, 100
    media and, 68
St. Mary's Industrial School for Boys,
    24–25
Sammy Claus. See Sosa, Sammy
Sammy So-So. See Sosa, Sammy
San Francisco Giants, 82, 99
Schamberger, Katherine (Ruth's
    mother), 24
Schilling, Curt, 67
Seattle Mariners, 67, 80
Selig, Allan "Bud," 58–59, 82
Seybold, Socks, 28
Sosa, Juan (brother), 74–75
Sosa, Kenia (daughter), 78
Sosa, Keysha (daughter), 78
Sosa, Luis (brother), 75
Sosa, Michael (son), 78
Sosa, Sammy, 10–11, 68, 100
    as "Sammy Claus," 84
    awards of, 82–83
    background of, 74–75
    Cubs and, 76–79, 82
    Esther and, 77
    home runs and, 78–82, 85–90
    Hurricane Georges and, 83–84
    McGwire and, 69–71, 80–82

media and, 80
minor leagues and, 75–76
1997 season and, 78–79
personality of, 73–74, 80–81
White Sox and, 76
Sosa, Sammy, Jr. (son), 78
South Atlantic league, 52
Spahn, Warren, 53
Stallard, Tracy, 46
Stengel, Casey, 39
Stevens, Julia, 28
sticker (hitter), 13
Stovey, George, 17
Sultan of Swat. See Ruth, George
    Herman "Babe"
Sylvester, Johnny, 32

Tampa Bay Devil Rays, 86
Terrell, Walt, 63
Texas Rangers, 75–76
Thomas, Frank, 76
Thomson, Bobby, 53
Thorpe, Jim, 20
Tiger Stadium, 80
Time magazine, 81
Topping, Dan, 40–41
town ball (game), 13
Trachsel, Steve, 70
Tree. See McGwire, Mark
Turner Field, 48

University of Oklahoma, 37
University of Southern California, 62

Vaughn, Ron, 62
Vega, Bernardo, 84
Ventura, Robin, 76
Vidmer, Richard, 29
Virgil, Ozzie, 75

Walker, Moses Fleetwood, 17
Walker, Tilly, 9
Walker, William Welday, 17
Warhop, Jack, 27
Washington, George, 14
Washington Senators, 40–41
Williams, Billye, 56
Williams, Ken, 31
Williams, Ted, 41
Williams College, 15, 98
Williamson, Ned, 28, 98

Wilson, Hack, 40–41, 70
Wood, Kerry, 79
Woodford, Helen, 26–27, 31
World Series, 27
    Aaron and, 54
    beginnings of, 17
    exhibitions and, 31
    Maris and, 40, 46
    New York Yankees and, 29
    of 1903, 98
    of 1918, 28
    1919 scandal and, 20
    of 1926, 32

of 1932, 23, 32
of 1958, 55
of 1968, 47
    Oakland and, 64
Wright, Harry, 15
Wrigley Field, 32, 69, 82

Xaverian Brothers, 24–25

Yankee Stadium, 9, 35, 44, 47, 63
York, Rudy, 80

Zoss, Joel, 16

PICTURE CREDITS

ABOUT THE AUTHOR

This is the ninth book written by Michael V. Uschan. His previous works for Lucent include a biography of golfer Tiger Woods, *Male Olympic Champions, The Importance of John F. Kennedy,* and *America's Founders.* Mr. Uschan began his career as a writer and editor with United Press International, a wire service that provides stories to newspapers, radio, and television. Because journalism is sometimes called "history in a hurry," he considers writing history books a natural extension of skills he developed as a journalist. While a reporter for UPI, Mr. Uschan wrote stories about Hank Aaron's final years with the Milwaukee Brewers. The author still covers sports for the Associated Press, including Brewers baseball games. He and his wife, Barbara, live in Franklin, Wisconsin, a suburb of Milwaukee.